DISCARD

3/18 last 11/19 jm 6/20

CALIFORNIA CONTEMPORARY

CALIFORNIA CONTEMPORARY

THE HOUSES OF GRANT C. KIRKPATRICK AND KAA DESIGN

PRINCETON ARCHITECTURAL PRESS, NEW YORK

CONTENTS

THIS BOOK IS DEDICATED TO MY BROTHER KENT, WHO LEFT THIS BEAUTIFUL PLANET WAY TOO EARLY.

PREFACE

Residential design is the most personal and powerful platform for architecture to affect our lives. We know this because the word *home* is powerful for all of us. I am a third-generation Californian who grew up on the Palos Verdes Peninsula, about fifteen miles south of Los Angeles. My earliest memories of home are of the land: rolling hills, views of the city sprawling out below, and nature everywhere. My father had a real job, but his true passion was taking care of the two acres of land we lived on. He saw in it the color, texture, and sounds of nature. I saw it as mowing, weeding, and irrigation repair. The work did pay fifty cents a week, but what I didn't yet perceive were the values that this time in the garden would imprint so deeply on my psyche—values so powerful that they form the very essence of how I view the world, and my work, today. They define my connection to nature, and that informs the way I see beauty.

Architecture chose me when I was a young kid and my parents remodeled their traditional ranch house on this property. My fascination was piqued the night I borrowed the contractor's plans and drew all over them. The next day, after a stern lecture, my dad introduced me to two elements of what would become my whole world: a drafting table and stool. That was it: architecture would be my manifestation of beauty. Later, when I went to the University of Southern California to study architecture, the connections between my passions for modern architecture and landscape design crystallized. I have traveled the world, and (much to my wife and kids' chagrin) our trips are mostly architectural and wine-region junkets. But I have always returned to Southern California, situating my firm and my family near the beach, where the light is sublime, the optimism abundant, and the lifestyle untethered.

Since beginning my independent practice in 1988 in a small shop near the Santa Monica Freeway, I have designed hundreds of houses across California and beyond, and with two partners and staff of roughly thirty-five have built KAA Design into one of the largest residential architecture and landscape design firms in the state. But it is California's imprint that deserves the credit for the houses I design. I am blessed to be living in this spectacular climate, where a love of nature can be nurtured like nowhere else.

I am grateful for the many collaborations that have allowed me to exercise this passion. And although I have never done the same thing twice, after thirty years of creating homes, this book provided the opportunity to depict the unique ideals that inform my work. The introduction, "The Nature of Nature," describes my background and philosophy though the lens of our ranch and vineyard in Central California. Part One illustrates the six principles of my design through examples representing more than thirty KAA houses. Part Two showcases six homes to tell their entire story.

My hope is that you pour yourself a nice glass of Syrah, put on a little music, and share in some of the beauty that we are drawing from this golden land of dreams.

—Grant C. Kirkpatrick, 2017

THE NATURE OF NATURE

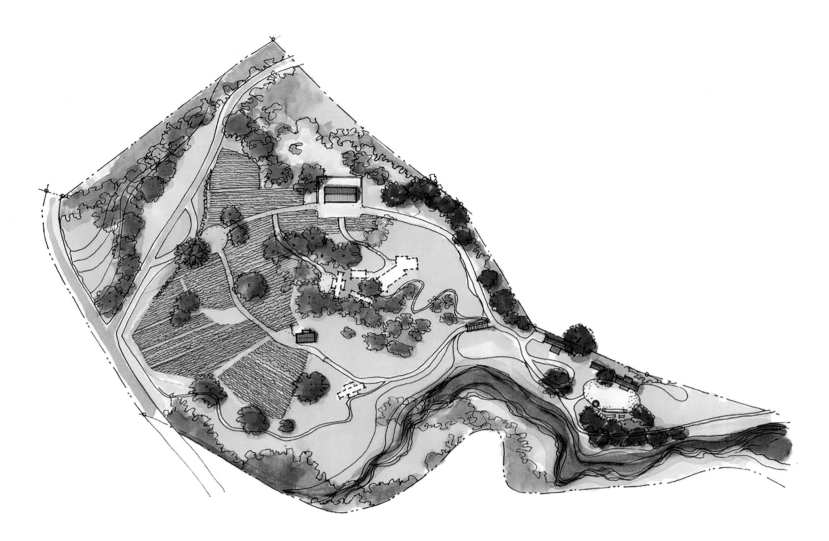

A place where we could get dirty, where we could be outside all day and into the night…a family retreat while our kids were growing up…a place where friends and family could visit and do old-school things like play horseshoes, lounge in hammocks and swings, pass lazy hours on the dock, throw big cookouts, and put on talent shows in the evening…a place to connect with nature.…This is what my wife, Shaya, and I wanted, for ourselves and for our kids. We knew how we wished to live; what we didn't know was where. And so we began our search, one that lasted for years. And when we found the property, we bought it. Sight unseen. That's how Split Rock Ranch came to be.

The first time I saw the land, I was with my son Jack. Together, we made the four-hour trek north from our home in Los Angeles to have a close look at the property, which sits on the shores of Lake Nacimiento in Central California. As we hiked all around the thirty acres, filled with pine trees and old—very old—majestic oaks, we couldn't quite believe it was ours. The property was completely undeveloped and in need of a lot of TLC; at one point, I even wondered, What have I done? But that feeling didn't last long. Beyond the neglect, I saw nothing but opportunity. Through the years, little by little, we would befriend nature and make the land ours.

PREVIOUS PAGES: Split Rock Ranch is located on the shores of Lake Nacimiento, halfway between Los Angeles and San Francisco, in the Paso Robles wine region. ABOVE: The thirty-acre property encompasses two prefab homes, a four-acre vineyard, and a large barn, along with other outbuildings.

PREVIOUS PAGES AND LEFT: The gentle, rolling topography dotted with California oaks inspired the design of these prefab dwellings. Clad in Cor-Ten steel, a material derived from the earth and widely seen in agricultural areas, they feature redwood porches and Douglas fir doors and windows. Each house is surrounded by decks that hover over the varied terrain. ABOVE: The homes were factory built and trucked to the property 95 percent complete.

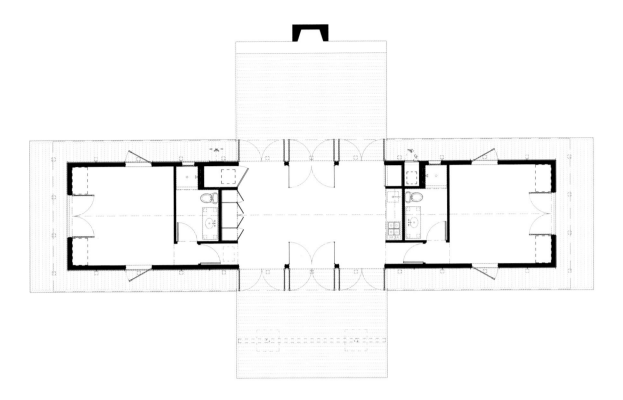

OVER TIME

As an architect, I spend my life looking at property, thinking about how the people who live there will use it and about how to connect them to their land. My goal is to help make the most of a place—to marry the residents' individual lifestyles to the specifics of that location. By weaving these two threads together, I discover the story of the project, which informs the ultimate vision and the design direction. Now it was time to do the same for myself and my family, to test my theories and use my design experience to create this connection for us in this particular place.

Split Rock Ranch wasn't about building a house on a property but rather about allowing the structures to develop organically into a village. And stewardship of the land and the surrounding nature was the key. This meant finding ways to design in harmony with our land—to make it better than before. We were seeking something else, too—not only a place but also a legacy for our family and hopefully for generations to come. All of that was well and good, and we were eager to start. But first, to make this project work, I had to figure out a way to keep things manageable. I accepted that any plan for building Split Rock Ranch had to include the words *over time*.

We started by clearing the land where trees had fallen, tending to areas that had been long neglected, and developing spots that caught the morning sunrise or that nurtured special views of the rock outcroppings, trees, or the lake. And we cultivated the spaces in between, creating seating areas, hammock groves, and picnic areas in the dappled light of the oaks, always with the idea that outdoor living was as important as indoor living.

The central living area reveals the focus of the two-bedroom, two-bath homes: simplicity, transparency, sustainability. Constructed with environmentally sensitive and FSC-certified materials, including cork floors, the dwellings feature site-built decks on each side. The uphill deck is anchored by a Cor-Ten steel fireplace that serves as a setting for outdoor dining. At just one thousand square feet, the homes encourage family togetherness and easy indoor-outdoor living.

The first thing we built was a dock, which might seem surprising for an architect who has designed residences for thirty years. But the dock made the first part of our plan work; each morning, we would boat over to "day camp" from a rental house across the lake from our property. We'd picnic and work on a project while the kids would happily go about getting dirty. At night we'd either camp out or head back across the lake.

Soon came the motor homes. Friends would gather, and we'd circle the RVs. These were the first of our annual multifamily summer gatherings at the lake.

Then the first prefab home was born. I loved the idea of living lightly on the land and making a minimal footprint on nature's platform. There would be no large retaining walls, no outsize lawn or pool in our plans. In addition, we realized that it would be difficult to get building resources to the property, given its somewhat remote location. With that in mind, I set about looking at factory-built or prefab homes that could be built efficiently off-site and, ideally, would hover above the land on light foundations.

Fortuitously, my family and I had recently returned from visiting friends in New Zealand, where we were enchanted by the getaway homes called *baches* and the lifestyle that goes with them. Though small in size, these iconic vacation houses at the beach or up in the mountains hold a big place in Kiwis' minds and hearts, as they head out often to their simple weekend retreats. Back in California, I set about creating with my design team a line of beautiful and easily constructed factory homes, and I was excited to make Split Rock the prototype location.

The Lake House was our first prefab to make it up the long, winding roads behind a very slow-moving semi. The house's placement gave us a great view of the lake, and setting it next to one particularly large oak tree offered the afternoon shade we needed. The Lake House cantilevers off the land in the front and tucks into the land at the back; that's where we put a small concrete wall with a steel fireplace. I'm not sure what I love more: the juxtaposition of the rusting steel and poured concrete, so simple and clean, or the way this terrace instantly became everyone's favorite gathering spot well into the cool evenings. It is the true hearth of the ranch.

We inserted the second prefab home, the Tree House, into a grove of oaks not far away. Wedging it among the trees required a little more of a surgical approach, but now, seeing how the trees frame the house and watching one tree grow up through the deck, it's clear that it was worth the effort. This house gives us a "nestled in nature" feeling of well-being and repose. Our village was beginning to come to life.

A few summers later, we held a barn raising in a big, open valley that's part of the vineyard we later built. This structure was intended to house all of the equipment for the ranch, but it quickly became the setting for evening and sometimes late-night events. Sure enough, the barn was soon dubbed the "Barty"; we subsequently outfitted its interior with a three-bedroom, two-bathroom suite to accommodate more guests.

Throughout the property, nature-inspired texture stories abound; the corrugated-steel panels and the raw-wood architectural details reflect the organic in the environment. A solar-heated outdoor shower offers a blend of freedom and shelter, as do the eaves and floating decks of each dwelling.

As time passes in our family's rural village, I'm seeing our story of living simply unfold more clearly. It's happening through the marriage of the village to the land and the elements, the wind and the sun and the trees—oh, those magnificent California oaks, which give our place such character, longevity, and timelessness. The oaks have contributed so much to our story, hosting hammocks, swings, gathering spots, and even a "lamp forest" that casts warm light over our long picnic table.

My eye is always searching for the perfect view, whether inside or outside a home, and it has been no different at Split Rock. Up at one end of our property, on the hill overlooking the lake, is a spot that we call Inspiration Point. From our seating area on that hill, at the end of a big day, just as the sun is sinking below the horizon, we watch its rays shine down the lake and reflect off the water. For a couple of minutes, the water turns a glittering pink. It's a beautiful phenomenon that's become part of our Split Rock story, as my daughter, Allie, and I have established a ritual (or maybe a competition): the first one who yells "Pink water!" wins. Until the next day…

PREVIOUS PAGES AND ABOVE: The silver corrugated-aluminum barn contrasts with the green of the vineyard. The large sliding barn doors are made of Cor-Ten steel frames and tension rods. The barn contains a two-story, three-bedroom, two-bath "condo" and functional storage space for agricultural machinery. But more often than not, it doubles as a lively entertaining space, earning its moniker "the Barty." OPPOSITE: A bit of happenstance provides a moment of respect for nature as the unexpected exposed bedrock becomes the foundation for the concrete retaining wall that follows the slope of the hill.

THE FARMER

The guiding principle behind Split Rock is the idea that when human beings and nature work together, it's possible to create something more extraordinary than either could alone. This collaboration is one that plays a role in everything I design.

The roots of this idea were planted deep within me from an early age. Every weekend in Rolling Hills, California, where I grew up, my two brothers and I worked alongside my father taking care of our two acres of land. Both my dad and my grandfather were lawyers by trade, but they were also farmers who took pride in working the land themselves. I inherited their sense of stewardship. Like them, I take great pride in caring for my land (and hope that one day my children will, as well).

So perhaps it's not surprising that I wanted to find even more ways for Split Rock to reflect this collaboration between humans and nature. On gracefully rolling hills, in a clearing with perfect sun and soil, I planted a vineyard. With help from many experts, we decided upon a trellised vineyard that would span four acres. This marked the beginning of our ten-year journey to the first vintage, a journey that has only added to my love of this land and to my farming legacy.

In addition to pride, anyone who has worked the land also earns a sense of humility. Nature is both beauty and beast, at once malleable and unpredictable. Each season in the vineyard brings new challenges. And out of those challenges come a deeper connection to and respect for the land. What began as an outgrowth of my love for and fascination with wine has evolved far beyond that. Building and tending the vineyard has allowed me to understand, through a very personal experience, the strong emotional connection people have with their property.

PREVIOUS PAGES AND OPPOSITE: The juxtaposition of the natural terrain and the rolling grid of vines is the ultimate expression of the connection between man and nature. The vine rows make way for centuries-old California oaks. FOLLOWING PAGE: A one-hundred-year-old Aermotor windmill, found entirely disassembled in a Paso Robles junkyard, presides over the growing grapes.

Block 1A

Syrah

.36 acres

492 plants

SPLIT ROCK
RANCH

THE MARRIAGE OF CONTRASTS

At the root of the connection between human beings and nature are contrasts and juxtapositions. My professional medium is contemporary architecture; I like clean lines and straight angles. Yet I'll always have a deep and abiding love for the curving, imperfect, moving lines that are inherent in nature. The vineyard offers just such a contrast and marriage: a grid of vines, spaced evenly in each direction, ranges over the bucolic, undulating hills. Organic and sinuous, orderly and precise, the land rises and falls in a dance of crisscrossing vines soaking up the sun.

Every spring we anticipate seeing the rows of bright green alfalfa push up between the dormant brown vines. In summer the ground reverses to brown while the vines dress themselves in a rich, lush green. In that same small valley, I never tire of seeing the contrast of the silvery side of the barn and the green vines. Nearby, there's a concrete retaining wall embedded into the bedrock, mimicking the natural slope of the land.

From the deck of the Lake House, I catch sight of another playful juxtaposition: the dancing lamps suspended from the canopy of trees. We chose to hang the lamps in a random pattern, symbolic of another overarching goal of mine—to create moments that feel on the one hand purposeful and on the other hand organic.

Being at this ranch has honed my appreciation for nature as the canvas where all of the principles of my design work are at play. There are qualities I seek to achieve on every project—a seamless relationship between the indoors and outdoors and architecture that pleases the eye and inspires the viewer—and tools I consistently use to do so: indigenous materials that reflect the surrounding environment. Then there are the ingredients that make Split Rock unique: the way structures rise over the land and capture particular vistas, the individual exterior and interior details that have been lovingly crafted by hand, the whimsy and imperfection of this place at this time for these people—family, friends, and me. And woven through it all are common threads: enough intrigue, variety, and surprise to keep things interesting; enough solidity, structure, and order to make things reassuring, calming, timeless. All of us are seeking something transcendent in our homes. Our connection to nature—constantly changing and evolving, yet primal, abiding, eternal— is always the platform on which this transcendence unfolds.

The land and our stewardship of it. Family, friends, and good times together. Time spent under the canopy of trees, overlooking the lake, watching bald eagles soar. And when the grapes ripen and we bottle our wine, my hope is that everyone who spends time with us here has those same feelings of well-being, feelings that pour over us when people and nature come together in one dynamic, lively, and exquisite blend.

A constellation of varied lamps—all made of nautical rope—expresses the organic magic at Split Rock Ranch.

PART ONE
THE IDEALS

I was once asked what I would buy first for a completely empty home. My answer was a bonsai tree. With dedication and care, it can grow into something even more beautiful, soothing, and inspiring than it would otherwise have been. This idea—that human beings and nature can be better together—forms the root of all of my design work, and the tree is an apt metaphor for my overall approach.

TRANSCENDENT IDEALS form the structure—the trunk of the tree—of every project. No matter where a home is set or who will live there, I envision it with materials that are indigenous and appropriate for its setting, paired with structural materials whose hard work is revealed. Seamless living is essential, with gracious, frequent, and effortless connections between the indoors and outdoors so the residents can enjoy both as much as possible. And every home requires careful attention to form and scale—shapes and volumes that are pleasing to the eye, with interior and exterior spaces that feel comfortable and accessible for real people. These principles give a home universal appeal and a sense of timelessness.

HUMANISTIC IDEALS form the branches and canopy of the tree. These are what distinguish each home, giving it a one-of-a-kind character and reflecting the residents' passions, inspirations, and even sense of humor. Touches of whimsy and imperfection, handcrafted elements, and a sense of levitation elevate the experience of home beyond the everyday.

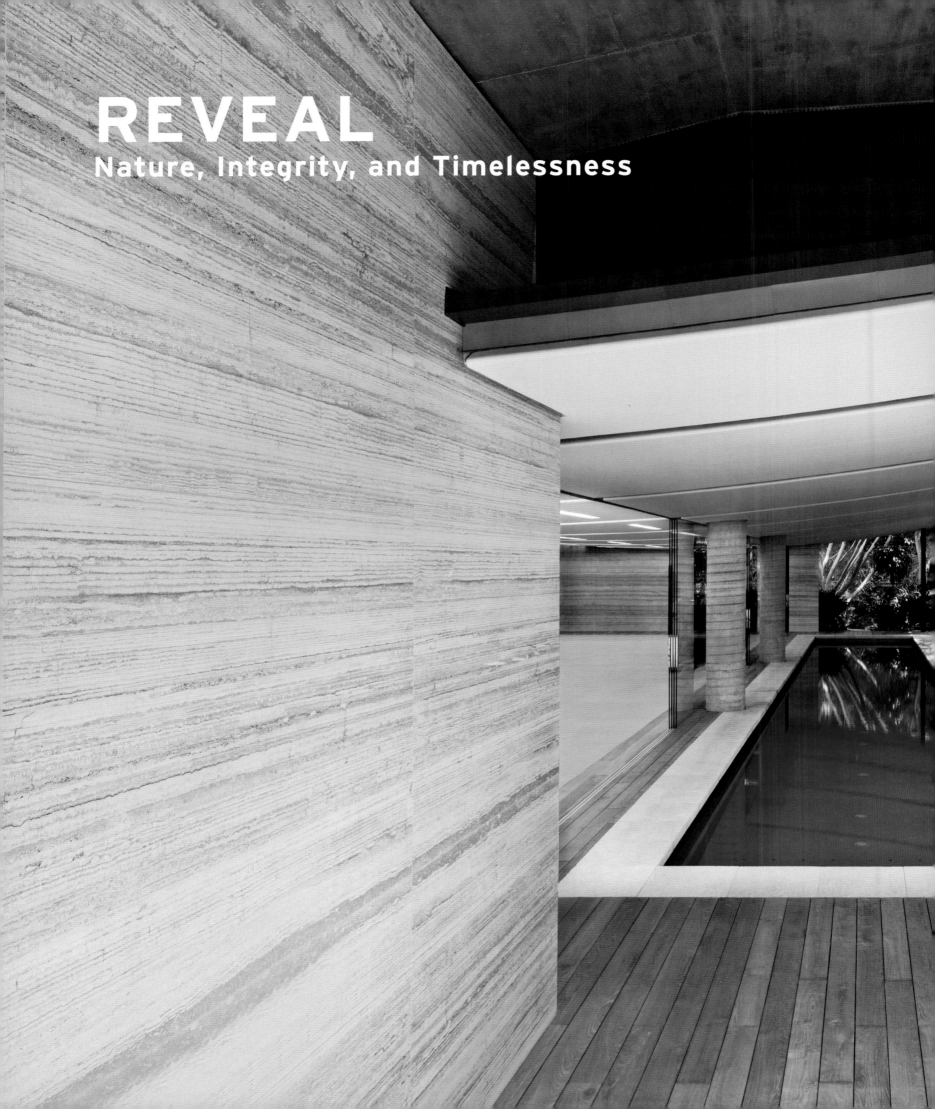

REVEAL
Nature, Integrity, and Timelessness

In wine making, the word *terroir* means much more than just the earth in which the grapes are grown. While the soil—the foundation for the vines—is key, *terroir* also means the topography of the land and the surrounding climate. A home and its natural environment are inextricably linked, and local materials offer a sense of authenticity that feels right.

Each of my design choices is guided by the belief that the most timeless and transcendent homes are also the most genuine and honest. That is why I always assemble the architectural palette by using indigenous materials, revealing the home's structure, and incorporating a range of textures.

Today we have incredible access to materials from all over the world, but when we choose to build as our ancestors did—to cast the home out of what surrounds it—the result seems natural, elemental. Near the coast, woods such as mahogany or cedar are comfortable and suitable for dwelling in moist climates. Limestone and sandstone reflect the beach. Even the man-made structural materials in a home can complement the setting: for example, concrete walls that have been poured using wooden molds have a texture that echoes driftwood.

Exposing the steel beams, the concrete walls, and the wood columns that support a home and form its structure is another means of communicating "This place is real." Instead of covering these elements, we reveal them and the hard work they perform. The way a design celebrates the juxtaposition of tactile and visual textures—industrial concrete with glimmering bronze, honed stone pavers next to a rough-hewn wall, rusticated reed ceilings supported by smooth mahogany columns—contributes enormously to the warmth and beauty of the home, reminding us of the endless combinations of textures and materials found in nature.

PREVIOUS PAGES AND OPPOSITE: The open plan welcomes abundant natural light and cooling breezes in this dynamic home gym and spa. An unexpected oasis beneath an existing tennis court, the partial indoor-outdoor area is formed with cleft natural stone walls, sandblasted concrete columns, travertine walls, reclaimed Indonesian teak floors, and white plaster ceilings.

OPPOSITE: A board-formed concrete wall serves as a backdrop to the patinated-bronze entry door and mahogany ceiling at the main entrance. BELOW: The integral-color concrete wall highlights the natural grain and knots of the wood forms.

RIGHT: Mahogany takes center stage at the juncture of the two adjoining wings, where a flared roof poses on soaring columns. Warm-toned, smooth plaster—troweled by hand-sets the backdrop for the richly colored wood. FOLLOWING PAGES, LEFT: Nature provides an inspirational palette of materials: the sculptural tree, the dark rock, and the patterned concrete wall provide a place for contemplation. FOLLOWING PAGES, RIGHT: Wood screens, trellises, and louvers are key textural elements that filter light, enhance privacy, and control exposure to and from the outside.

The middle of this home opens up both
vertically to the sky and horizontally to
lush gardens and vistas. Mahogany, plaster,
and stone capture and reflect light and
tie the interior spaces to the outdoors.

The architectural and landscape materials take a cue from the Pennisetum grasses on the beach outside (below) and the horsetail reeds inside the courtyard (opposite).

Varied and enduring natural and man-made materials evoke permanence and respond to their context. Here, coastal retreats reflect sand, ocean, and horizon.

WEAVE
Seamless Indoor-Outdoor Living

I grew up in an old ranch house, which my parents had remodeled into a distinctly modern home. In addition to enjoying its views and connection to the gardens, they frequently entertained, throwing open the windows and doors to let guests wander in and out, enjoying the light and the mild weather. To me, a house that is open to nature is a friendly house, a lived-in house. Call me a native Californian, but I can't imagine living any other way.

And I'm not alone in this. Every home I create is designed to seamlessly connect the indoors and outdoors. I am always thinking about how the architecture can bring the residents closer to nature. There are so many ways to do this, especially in as hospitable a climate as Southern California's. Everyone loves outdoor rooms, such as terraces adjacent to living areas. I've also designed outdoor foyers, where guests enter the home through a gate and immediately discover a view through floor-to-ceiling windows to the sea beyond. And at my own house, a *palapa* with a sturdy ceiling of reeds offers just enough shelter while we spend time trading stories next to the fireplace in the fresh night air.

I place a priority on opening rooms up to the air, the light, and the views. I sometimes say that instead of putting windows in our walls, our walls are windows. And doors, for that matter. These disappearing walls (including doors that slide or fold away) not only allow activity to flow inside and out but also enhance the indoor experience, providing views and directing light into the house. For the ultimate feeling of luxury, I've designed numerous spa bathrooms that open up to the elements on three sides, as well as living rooms sheltered by louvered doors that seem to melt away, revealing pure ocean stretching to the horizon. When a home has spectacular views of the ocean, the city, or the hills beyond, it feels natural to maximize these sight lines. When inspiring views aren't a given, creating them becomes an intriguing challenge. It's not uncommon for me when designing a home on a lot that is small, as many are in the coastal communities, to incorporate an organic-feeling interior view, such as a courtyard anchored by a fountain and lush greenery—a welcome pause between private spaces like the bedrooms and public spaces like the living room.

Glowing fires (flickering in a fireplace or ascending toward the sky from fire pits or hurricane lanterns) and murmuring water (circulating gently in a koi pond, running through a rock in a courtyard, or even channeled through a living room) serve as visual focal points and magnets for gatherings, reminding us, on a primal level, of the pleasure of being in nature yet protected, cozy, and in control of our domain.

Another versatile tool is the clerestory window. Placed along the top of a wall, these small, rectangular windows allow wonderful air flow, especially when they face each other on opposite sides of a room. They also offer precious views of the sky, but because they are high up, they don't compromise the inhabitants' privacy. And as a bonus, the light that filters through them at night causes a lantern effect that is incredibly inviting for visitors or residents returning home.

It gives me a lot of joy to build homes that people love living in. It gives me even more joy when those homes also connect the owners with nature—or even deepen their love of it.

PREVIOUS PAGES: An inviting seating area around a circular fire pit provides expansive city views. The green roof of this eco-conscious home uses indigenous grasses and plants as a foreground to the urban vista beyond. OPPOSITE: Inside and outside blend effortlessly in this beach room, which can be closed off or opened completely to the elements. The pool with fountain connects the space to the horizon, even when enclosed by louvered doors that control sunlight and provide privacy from the busy boardwalk and bike path.

The main entry is on the middle
level of this home. The adjoining
upper and lower levels are
tied together around a daylit
garden. The space features an
artist-commissioned fountain
made from a granite boulder.

The color and materials palette extend this great room onto a terrace that serves as the home's outdoor living room. Limestone flooring, large sliding-door openings, and a fireplace as focal point weave indoors and outdoors into one.

This home's design evolved from the landscape plan, instead of the other way around. Floor-to-ceiling, wall-to-wall glass doors slide open on both sides of the great room, where living and dining areas straddle two adjacent gardens.

RIGHT: Floor-to-ceiling glass doors allow for the airy space to connect with the sun, sea, and horizon beyond. FOLLOWING PAGES, LEFT: A two-story glass foyer leads to the entry courtyard beyond. The serpentine wood louver system above filters the sunlight and provides privacy. FOLLOWING PAGES, RIGHT: A folding glass door system ties the living room and garden areas together (top left). The screened upstairs balcony provides privacy and sun control while allowing cross-ventilation (top right). Clerestory windows atop the concrete wall create a welcoming lantern-like effect at the entry (bottom right). A horizontal clerestory window frames the garden foliage while maintaining privacy for the bedroom (bottom left).

Clerestory windows and a folding glass door system allow complete indoor-outdoor flow in this living space.

A front-row beachside location calls for a seamless connection with the outdoors. The master bedroom suite's floor-to-ceiling glass doors pocket away out of view, while the balcony preserves privacy from the well-traveled bike path below.

SCULPT
Form, Scale, and Proportion

We have an instinctive sense of what is pleasing to our eyes. Whether it's the lines of a classic car, the elegant curve of a grand piano, or the familiar pitch of a gabled roof, we recognize attractive shapes and interesting lines. Our Goldilocks instinct also lets us know when a space or a place feels just right—whether a room will be comfortable before we even sit down, or whether the front of a home is designed to invite or impress. In design, these qualities of form and scale go hand in hand.

This harmony of form and scale is so ingrained in my design work that it has become part of my subconscious. I seek it instinctively so that I can provide my clients with the same kind of delighted recognition I felt when I went to Fallingwater for the first time. Two main aspects of Frank Lloyd Wright's masterwork resonated strongly with me: the way the parts come together in a masterful whole (especially the way the horizontal and vertical elements play off each other) and the scale of the home in relation to what's around and inside it—the river, the trees, the furniture. There's a wonderful sense of variety, and yet everything coheres.

Variety and contrast—my old friends—are fundamental to why Fallingwater affects us the way it does, and both play an important role in designing buildings with good form and scale. In my own work, I often look for ways to break a home into intriguing shapes rather than treating it as one solid mass. To make the scale feel right, I liberally pair horizontals, which ground us and suggest permanence, with verticals, which inspire us and suggest uplift and optimism. Creating a collection of smaller, interconnected sections, which I sometimes call "pavilionizing," can make a large home look and feel almost like a village that has grown organically, on an agreeable and comfortable human scale.

Inside the home, these pairings of form and scale continue. I combine the right angles I love with the occasional sinuous curve, which draws the eye through the space, blending what is otherwise clean and organized with a refreshing asymmetry and sense of surprise. These juxtapositions promote an appealing tension: the home becomes both restful and energizing.

PREVIOUS PAGES: This home is a collection of vertical volumes arranged in a village-like ensemble with panoramic views. OPPOSITE: Varying planes of materials, such as mahogany, hand-troweled plaster, and concrete, generate dynamic shadows as the sunlight changes.

PREVIOUS PAGES: This expansive facade—flanked by two smooth plaster volumes and wood-sided walls—appears symmetrical at first glance. Closer inspection reveals a playful asymmetry, as seen in the louvered second-story volume and entry toward the center, emphasized by a glowing cantilevered roof. The facade employs horizontal clerestories that offset the slender vertical windows on both levels, reflecting the varying functions within.

RIGHT: The entry is flanked by thicker stone volumes that slightly chamfer upward to draw in natural light and emphasize texture. Wood siding and horizontal and vertical bands of glass further carve the home into pleasing proportions.

BELOW, LEFT: The organic, sinuous stair provides an inviting counterpoint to the rigorously geometric plan. BELOW, RIGHT: Clerestory windows graze the ceiling with natural light, while the hard and soft materials delineate human scale. OPPOSITE: In this three-story home, each level is layered with a unique texture: limestone on the ground level, hand-troweled plaster on the middle level, and driftwood-colored cedar at the top.

PREVIOUS PAGES: The home as a village: pavilions share an intimate scale and material, but also define individual areas of the residence. Outdoor elements, including garden terraces and bridges, connect the buildings to each other and to nature.
RIGHT: On the second level, wood volumes containing the three children's bedrooms balance the expansive plaster facade.

DELIGHT
Whimsy and Imperfection

Each of us has a unique personality and passions, and sometimes we do the unexpected. The most inviting homes are like this, too. In addition to being beautiful and comfortable, they have an unforgettable character and offer us moments of delight and surprise, just like the people we love spending time with. I find that the surest way to achieve these qualities in a home is by incorporating touches of whimsy and imperfection.

Whimsical moments remind us of the endless discoveries and excitement we experienced as children. This might mean including a delicious little secret for the inhabitants, such as a tunnel connecting favorite rooms in the house, or it might mean turning a surfboard into a light fixture that hangs over a pool table, eliciting a smile in the owners whenever they are in the room and signaling to visitors, "Here's what this family loves." Moments of whimsy take the edge off and invite residents and their guests to relax and enjoy themselves, no matter how large or impressive the home may be.

Purposeful imperfection has a similar effect. As my work has evolved, I've become less and less interested in the notion of perfection. Perfection can be boring. Instead of conveying individuality and a sense of place, perfection has a sameness that could be found absolutely anywhere. I strive to achieve a certain level of intentional imperfection. It's not easy to pull off—not just because I'm naturally a perfectionist but also because it requires some risk and certainly some confidence. For instance, I might bevel a concrete or stone wall so that it softly tapers toward the sea or the garden. The effect suggests natural wear, the kind you might find on a beachside home that's been buffed down by the salt air over many generations and that only becomes more precious and full of memories as time passes. Once, when a carefully selected boulder meant as the anchor for a courtyard split roughly in two as it was being craned in, I convinced the owner to leave it; we added running water through the crack to emphasize the imperfection and celebrate this fortuitous accident.

Memorable homes are designed to evolve with us. They are like our favorite people; we appreciate their character, in spite of their quirks and flaws—and sometimes even more because of them.

PREVIOUS PAGES: At this oceanfront home, a second-level garden with pool nods to the active and playful family lifestyle. A circular window at the pool bottom brings light and fun to the spa bathroom below. OPPOSITE: At the entry courtyard a statue of three dancing sheep hints at the owner's whimsical nature. FOLLOWING PAGES, LEFT: Bringing a hanging swing chair inside created a moment of lighthearted fun for children and grown-ups alike. FOLLOWING PAGES, RIGHT: Ship's lanterns, suspended on nautical rope and hung at asymmetrical intervals, hang in the four-story stairway (top left). The illusionary "lamp" is a two-dimensional fixture built into the wall (top right). This six-foot-tall watchman, which has traveled with the owners from previous homes, stands guard at the entry (bottom right). A set of Kelly Wearstler brass legs is a source of amusement and reflection (bottom left).

OPPOSITE: To offset the predominantly orthogonal architecture of this home, an undulating wood screen, visible behind the upper windows, was introduced. The curved form provides privacy from the street while generating dramatic shadows. BELOW: This boulder was selected as a natural focal element for the courtyard off the dining area. While the boulder was being craned in, it split into two pieces. After a bit of coaxing, the owner agreed to see this serendipity as an example of welcomed imperfection.

Juxtaposing the basement-level bowling alley and the wine room combined the owners' passions in one playful arena.

BELOW: The Zen-inspired entry garden offers an instant sense of calm. Each boulder represents one of the five Confucian virtues, as seen in the sketch at right. OPPOSITE: This home exercise and spa area was created beneath the existing tennis court. The white plaster ceiling gently bends upward to invite light and allow a view of the garden beyond.

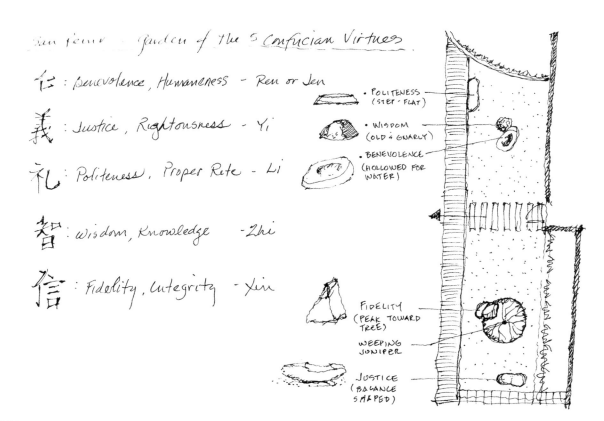

Zen garden - garden of the 5 Confucian Virtues

仁 : Benevolence, Humaneness - Ren or Jen

義 : Justice, Rightousness - Yi

礼 : Politeness, Proper Rite - Li

智 : Wisdom, Knowledge   - Zhi

信 : Fidelity, Integrity - Xin

• POLITENESS (STEP - FLAT)

• WISDOM (OLD & GNARLY)

• BENEVOLENCE (HOLLOWED FOR WATER)

FIDELITY (PEAK TOWARD TREE)

WEEPING JUNIPER

JUSTICE (BALANCE SHAPED)

OPPOSITE: The purposefully tapering stone wall emulates the natural erosion of masonry found in centuries-old seaside villages. BELOW: Sweeping curved pools reflect the azure sky above and draw one's eye to the ocean beyond. Rough stone coping and carved stone fire pits contrast with handmade cerulean mosaic pool tile.

CRAFT
Pride, Legacy, and Longevity

Craft has never been more essential than today. In our mass-produced world, it has almost become an art form. When we enter someone's home, we might be struck first by the obvious: high ceilings; a bright, sunny kitchen; a glowing pool in the backyard. But it's the details that form the individual character of the home and reflect the people who live there and what they appreciate.

Whether it's hand-laid stone flooring or an expertly crafted wood ceiling, our senses recognize one-of-a-kind objects, furnishings, and architectural elements and the care that went into making them. That's why I love working with craftspeople to create the defining layers of a home, inside and out. Many of the people I frequently collaborate with come from generations of artisans. They have so much pride in their work because it's not simply work; they believe in their craft, and they know it will in turn bring pride to the generations of families who will live in homes whose character has been shaped by handcrafted details.

That emphasis on the future is key because a true artisan strives not only for beauty but for longevity, too. He or she is always thinking about how to create something with staying power. For example, to bring concrete walls to life and make them feel residential instead of industrial, I often choose board-formed concrete. The molds are made with wood so that the final result has structural integrity as well as the natural beauty and variation of wood grain. It takes an expert to know how to do this right, and with concrete, there's only one shot—it's poured; it hardens; it's done. That means the process is important, of course, but it also means that if it's done well, you have something special and timeless surrounding you (and future generations) every day.

Similarly, the best woodworkers do more than offer lustrous finishes or interesting grains or stains. They ask, "What can be done to ensure there's no buckling or warping in the sea air? How can we make sure the wood breathes?" They help bring our creative design ideas to life, as well: Two different woods juxtaposed on a wall, one honey colored, light, and bright, the other rich, dark, and deep. An espresso-colored wood door with a glinting bronze handle. Details like these add warmth, life, and originality to the home.

And there's something incredibly soothing about being surrounded by elements or objects made by hand. It's a reminder that even in the modern world, we're still connected to the arts and crafts of the past. Handmade elements in our homes ground us as they balance the equal and opposite desire for our spirits to soar.

PREVIOUS PAGES: Revealing harmony: clean, simple forms of steel, glass, wood, and stone complement the dramatic horizon line of the Pacific Ocean. OPPOSITE: Concrete's inherent beauty is enhanced by sandblasted board forms.

PREVIOUS PAGES, LEFT: The artful use of the warm palette of materials demonstrates the careful collaborations of stonemasons, woodworkers, and plaster artisans. PREVIOUS PAGES, RIGHT: No front door necessary: a bronze-framed gate leads directly into the indoor-outdoor courtyard of this beach house. RIGHT: True craftsmanship means it's built to last. The way a home's materials are installed and treated has a powerful effect on the home's durability. It's important for clients to be able to enjoy their residences and not constantly worry about maintenance.

OPPOSITE: Stained wood paneling and contrasting windows highlight the fine line where materials come together (top left). A bronze plate surround delineates two tons of wood (top right). A steel lintel frames the opening to the concrete staircase beyond (bottom right). The theater door is clad in repurposed leather belts (bottom left). BELOW: Wooden stair treads are supported by a blackened steel beam and one-inch-diameter steel rods. FOLLOWING PAGES: A custom anodized aluminum gate and shutter system are combined with teak floor decking and board-formed concrete walls (left), while vertical-grained Douglas fir doors, siding, and eaves offer shelter on a limestone terrace (right).

Simple materials, including wood, stone, steel, and concrete,
work together to inspire and delight.

LEVITATE
Bridge, Cantilever, and Soar

If whimsy taps our funny bones, levitation taps our souls. We want to feel grounded in our homes—sheltered, safe, and comfortable. But we also want our homes to inspire us, to help us rise above the everyday. Architecture can literally and figuratively elevate us, lifting our spirits and allowing us to momentarily defy gravity. Honed throughout the years, my "levitation kit" is designed to do just that.

Bridges over courtyards or gardens, rooms or terraces that cantilever over the landscape, and roof eaves that extend like the finely tailored brim of a hat: in each of these cases, the architectural element is suspended with several sides free and unanchored in the open air, creating a sense of energy.

A bridge offers a dramatic moment of transition and suspension. Bridges are not often found in homes, but I love including them because traversing a space from above can be transformative. It engages our senses in a heightened way. Bridging works well on upper floors, both inside and outside, as well as in connecting various elements of the home or garden. Bridges can also mark the transition from indoors to outdoors, crossing over entry spaces, inviting us to leave daily cares and worries behind. We feel a brief sense of precariousness when the earth beneath us seems to slip away: our pulses quicken, our steps become a little more uncertain. And then the suspense passes—we know that what's beneath our feet is solid, after all—and a feeling of uplift and simple goodness remains.

Cantilevered structures have a similar effect. A cantilever is a horizontal platform or volume that is attached on only one side. Stairs suspended over a foyer; a balcony that extends over a stretch of the beach; a lounge deck above a swimming pool; a living space that hovers over a hillside above the city....These structures allow us to float above the world, as though we're on the prow of a ship. Surveying our domain from this vantage point promotes pride, awe, and inspiration from the beauty around us.

Eaves—the edges or corners of a roof—confirm that even when our feet are planted on terra firma, what we see can uplift us. As the uppermost part of a home, the roof offers a prime opportunity for conveying this idea of levitation. When eaves extend generously, like the wings of a bird, the house seems to take flight, reaching toward the horizon, soaring while protecting what's below from the rain and the sun. At night, when the light from within spills out below the eaves, the house glows. Our spirits lift: we are home.

PREVIOUS PAGES: Moments of levitation prompt a feeling of excitement and lightness: an upper terrace projects and hovers over the yard while an expansive daybed floats over the ground and above the pool. OPPOSITE: The blue water and the green garden are the only things visible from this reading nook in a window box suspended over the pool. Beyond, a floating daybed, submerged stepping stones, and a wood garden bridge all enhance the experience of levitation.

RIGHT: This cantilevered living room is the quintessential example of levitation. The main spaces of this residence thrust out and over the city like a prow of a great ship.
FOLLOWING PAGES: Dramatic cantilevering eaves also serve the practical function of protecting the spaces below from strong sunlight.

RIGHT: A raw-steel and wood stair floats against a backdrop of tactile warm stone. FOLLOWING PAGES, LEFT: Stair treads individually cantilever from the wall for a dynamic expression (top left). The subtly cantilevered structural supports provide a sense of shelter for the entry (top right). Steps of solid slabs of oak allow daylight to filter below (bottom right). This Japanese-inspired *roji* bridge offers a sense of repose at the entry garden (bottom left). FOLLOWING PAGES, RIGHT: The second-floor bridge pierces the two-story entry foyer, showcasing the marriage of varied materials with complementary patterns and textures.

A cantilevered stone pathway hovers over the garden as it leads from the street level to the main entry. The lighter-colored limestone stairs appear to float over the stone blocks beneath them.

PART TWO
WHERE THEY LIVE

Before I begin a project, I find the story, which always arises from a combination of the home's specific location and its future residents' lifestyle and needs. The marriage of the two forms the basis for an authentic story, a narrative from which everything then flows—from goals to design to the pragmatics of safety and maintenance. Many decisions arise organically from this process.

The six houses in the pages that follow reveal how we weave together our transcendent and humanistic principles to create beautiful, functional residences. These are homes that will last—not only because of how they were built but also because they can evolve with the people who live there. Art collectors and surfers, city dwellers and diehard seasiders: all want to live in a way that speaks authentically to their surroundings and graciously serves their everyday needs while elevating their spirits. These case studies illustrate these important principles, and as such, they reveal how our homes can become heirlooms.

SHIPSHAPE

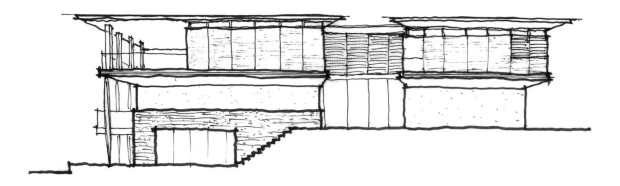

The two experienced sailors who live in this house have captained yachts and sailboats throughout their lives. It was only natural to envision their home as an ode to the couple's passion for oceangoing and the fine craftsmanship of wooden yachts. The property was perched on the edge of the Pacific Ocean, and the house was set to look like a boat nestling perfectly into the slip of a harbor. Every detail of the residence was informed by a nautical precision, designed to accommodate the specifics of the property and, of course, the beachfront conditions: wind (unpredictable), sun (extremely predictable), and sand (ever present, except in the home).

Overt and subtle maritime references answer practical needs and romantic desires. Floor-to-ceiling windows with water views pair with wood paneling indoors and out. The two-story-high mahogany columns on the ocean side of the house are actual ship masts. We commissioned sailboat craftsmen in Maine to execute the masts' design; I paired them with a custom shade system for the three-story house, with "sails" in the form of white panels of fabric that raise and lower to cut the wind and provide relief from the ocean glare, as well as to ensure privacy on this well-traveled public boardwalk.

On the second floor, a living room with louvered and bifold doors opens up completely to an unobstructed view of the ocean. This setting instantly transports the couple to the exhilaration of being on the rear deck of a yacht at sunset, when the spray is mild and the deepening colors of sea and sky dissolve into each other. And when the winds pick up in the evening, the owners can close the louvered doors and retreat to the "main cabin," where a fireplace and other creature comforts await.

The architectural palette is equally at home in this oceanfront environment. Board-formed concrete establishes the bulkhead at the beach level. Mahogany doors, windows, and louvered panels bring consistent warmth and craftsmanship throughout all three levels, and brass, bronze, and anodized-metal details will gracefully gain a patina in the sea air. Although permanently docked in its beachside berth, this vessel is shipshape in every way.

PREVIOUS PAGES: This home affords ocean views from all levels through various panoramic and framed apertures. The top floor contains the main living spaces, including a large, covered outdoor room with a view of the Pacific coastline. OPPOSITE: The beachfront facade is composed around four two-story, symmetrical mahogany "masts" beneath the top floor's covered terrace. Behind them, a purposeful asymmetry maintains ocean views and interior privacy for the midlevel master suite and boardwalk-level beach room. ABOVE: A concept sketch shows ship-like layers opening to the horizon at left. A board-formed concrete base establishes the bulkhead at the beach level, while the mahogany-clad top living floor floats above.

LEFT: Commissioned from ship craftsmen in Maine, the four slender ship masts connect the first and second stories of the house. Motorized white fabric panels reminiscent of sails offer glare protection and maintain privacy.

OPPOSITE: The steel floor rim of the home's living level cantilevers toward the horizon. Mahogany paneling, hand-troweled plaster, and board-formed concrete complete the palette.

BELOW: In contrast to the house's precise linear geometry, a circular staircase cuts a dramatic, sinuous swath through the center of the home, connecting the middle entry level with the top-floor living level. FOLLOWING PAGES, LEFT: The industrial nature of the structural concrete highlights the warm mahogany paneling. Recessed LED lighting reinforces the effect. FOLLOWING PAGES, RIGHT: At the entry a glimpse of the ocean surf beyond a linear garden beckons one to enter. At right, glass walls showcase the circular stair.

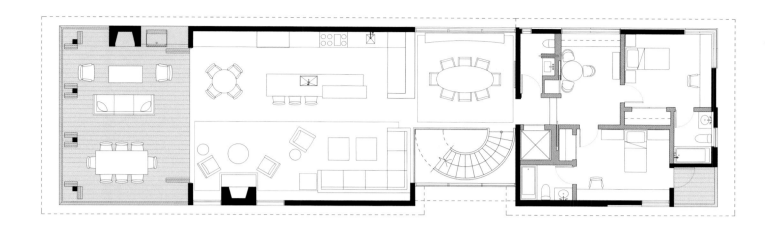

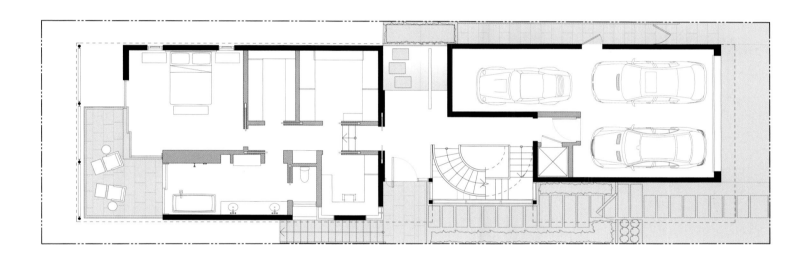

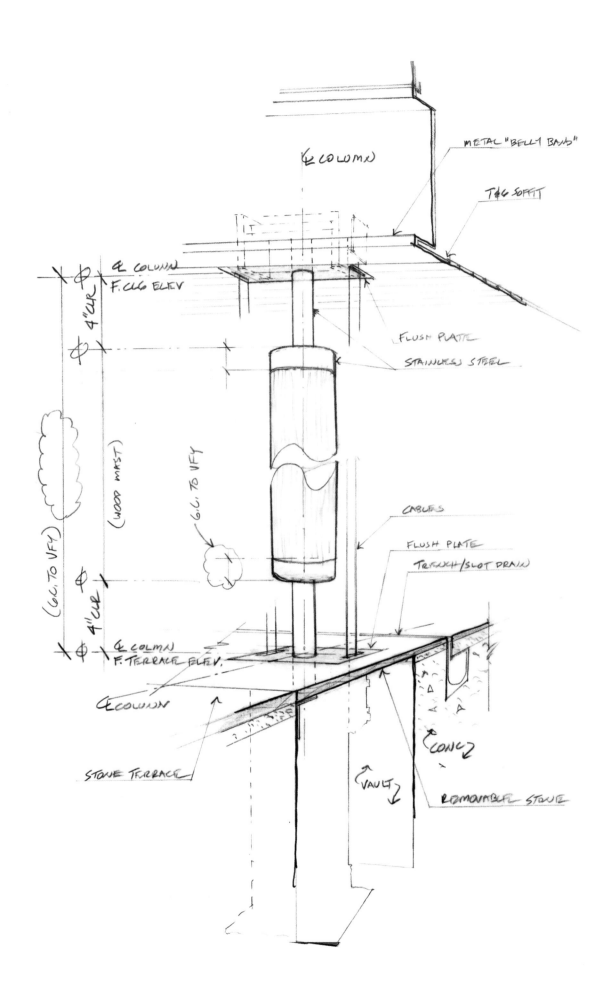

C COLUMN

METAL "BELLY BAND"

T&G SOFFIT

C COLUMN
F. CLG ELEV

4" CLR

FLUSH PLATE

STAINLESS STEEL

(WOOD MAST)

(GC. TO VFY)

GC. TO VFY

CABLES

FLUSH PLATE

TRENCH/SLOT DRAIN

4" CLR

C COLUMN
F. TERRACE ELEV.

C COLUMN

CONC

STONE TERRACE

VAULT

REMOVABLE STONE

PREVIOUS PAGES: Bifold bronze shutter doors, reminiscent of those in romantic ocean liners, frame striking horizon views. LEFT AND OPPOSITE: The deceptively simple concrete walls, bronze shutters, and mahogany columns are crafted with nautical precision. The motorized shade system was custom designed and engineered, with marine-grade motor and cable pulley systems.

A beach-level game room and pub flow directly outdoors via a four-panel pocketing mahogany door system.

Mahogany paneling and cabinetry combine with various metals throughout the home. The kitchen (below) integrates custom bronze details and hardware in an internal mahogany cabinet system. The entry and garage elevation (opposite) incorporates mahogany paneling, with anodized-steel detailing on the eaves, window shutters, cantilevered floor plate, and entry gates.

In the master suite, pocket doors and a private terrace prompt oceanside contemplation. A tailored composition of horizontal and vertical forms and quiet materials infuse the bedroom with a sense of calm (below). A sliding glass door at the edge of the master bath opens to a shaded balcony and the sunny beach beyond (opposite).

SAND STREETS

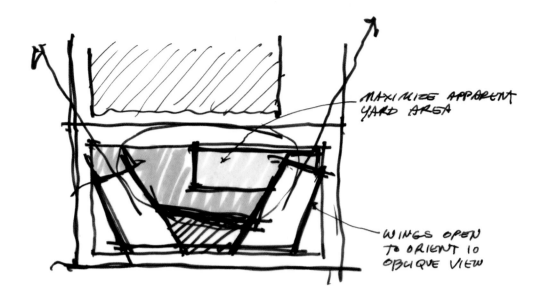

MAXIMIZE APPARENT YARD AREA

WINGS OPEN TO ORIENT TO OBLIQUE VIEW

Sometimes the stars align—along with the view, the property, and the client. Without a doubt, that happened with this home for a family of five. All of them are surfers, and some are serious about it; the oldest son and the father travel the world for surfing competitions.

It was clear that this house, just a few blocks from the beach, needed to support not only that surfer lifestyle but also that surfer life story: casual, open, and fun. We also knew we wanted the home to incorporate aspects of South Africa, where the father grew up. And so the attitude and the materials we chose evoke the South African palette and way of life translated to Southern California.

Few houses erase the line between inside and outside the way this one does. The entire top-floor living area feels like one large, continuous, luxurious modern camp. It's a space where you could just as easily have a relaxed, semi-open-air Thanksgiving as you could a laid-back *braai* (South African barbecue)—and both have taken place under its eucalyptus-reed ceiling.

The floor-to-ceiling windows are actually retractable doors that completely fold in on themselves to open up the space. And this is exactly how the family lives—not just opening those doors when guests come over, but keeping them open all day and night. The view of the ocean down the adjacent street gives them their own surf reports, updated moment by moment.

On the other side of the third floor, there's a different view, and this one continues to surprise the family. The owner expected to love her ocean view, of course, but at night, when the ocean is pitch black except for the occasional blinking lights of far-off oil tankers, she finds her bedroom view to be the one that pulls her in. Perched on her balcony, she looks southeast and sees the whole Palos Verdes Peninsula. There, the lights of individual houses in pocketed neighborhoods remind her that life is happening nearby and all around; that her family is safe and accounted for; and that tomorrow, when the morning light and surf come up, they'll be ready—without much effort at all—to meet both.

PREVIOUS PAGES: This home was designed as the setting for many layers of family activity: the walk street level hosts fun and play, beach access, and guest accommodations. The kids' bedrooms sit on the middle level. Designed for indoor-outdoor living, the top level, including the master suite, is capped by a floating reeded ceiling on exposed steel beams. ABOVE: An early concept sketch focuses the ocean views outward, toward the ends. OPPOSITE: Between the tapered stone walls, at the two-story entry, a custom South African wood screen enhances privacy and provides a glowing invitation at night.

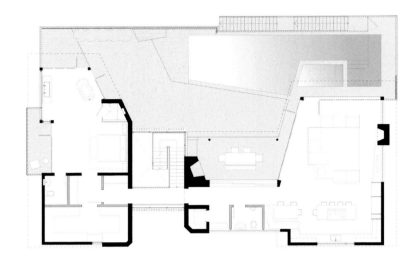

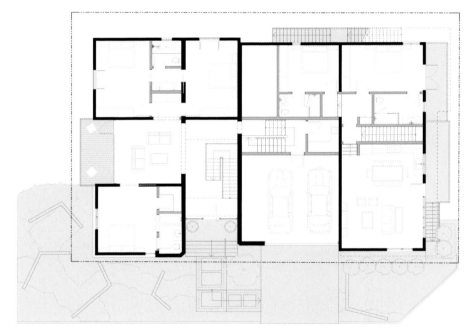

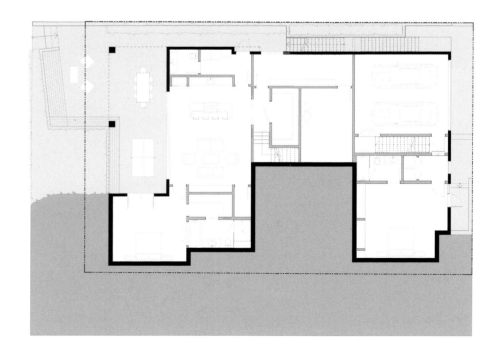

PREVIOUS PAGES: The home is bounded by a vehicular street and a public walk street used to access the beach by foot. Cedar planking and limestone rubble walls will patinate gracefully in the marine climate. OPPOSITE: The bedroom wing is executed with vertical wood siding and is capped with a floating roof.

The entry foyer features a floating stair to the upper, main living level and a bridge that connects the living areas to the master suite. Stone walls and a reeded ceiling accent the light and airy interior.

ABOVE: The unconventional top level balances open living space with exterior amenities, including a pool and spa, and lawn and deck areas. The living, kitchen, and dining areas are to the left, with the master suite on the far right. FOLLOWING PAGES, LEFT: The family frequently enjoys outdoor dining, complete with a *braai*, a South African barbecue. FOLLOWING PAGES, RIGHT: The organic palette of materials includes unskinned eucalyptus trunks as columns and skinned South African bamboo reeds for screens.

PREVIOUS PAGES: The multifunctional living space ensures seamless indoor-outdoor living. A ribbon of clerestory windows surrounds the upper level. OPPOSITE AND BELOW: The kitchen serves as a family and social space as much as an irresistible lure for the home cook. A center island with seating and a breakfast banquette tucked into the corner reinforce the home's casual, flexible design.

Located on the top level, the master suite is a unique private oasis. Bed and bath areas function as one, emphasizing spaciousness, flow, and abundant views of the garden and ocean beyond.

PACIFIC BELVEDERE

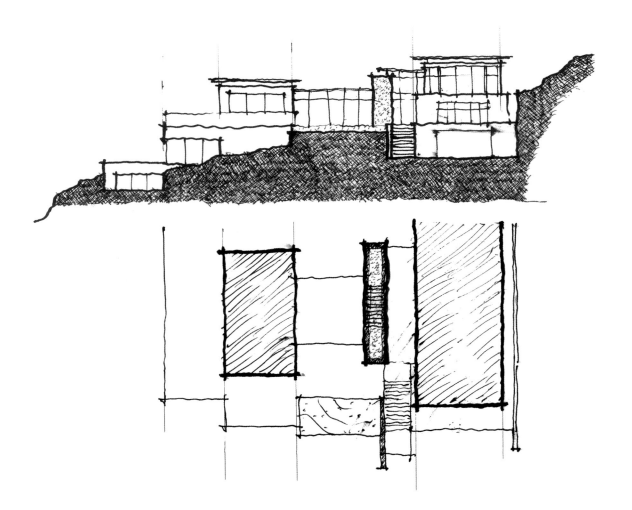

It's hard to forget my first visit to this property, a hilltop with a panoramic, almost 360-degree vista, perched high over the beautiful Del Mar community near San Diego. This was a summit, the kind of site where I am often requested to build "a castle on the hill." But this quaint Pacific Ocean beach-town setting—and fortunately, my clients—called for a different vision, one that took full advantage of the perch but was part of the neighborhood. That vision took form not as a house on the hill but as a house of the hill—a layered enclave that would engage its natural setting and offer indoor-outdoor moments that maximize views of the panorama beyond.

The original property, the former site of the water tower for the city below, was wild and unkempt. Our intention was to sculpt the house and landscape into and along the hillside, following its contours rather than jutting out from it. This resulted in as much planned space outdoors as indoors, which is just what's needed for this family with kids and a lot of friends they like to have over. Sports court, spa, outdoor bar, boccie court, outdoor kitchen—all of the outdoor features we designed for this house are used to their fullest capacity, and the layered approach allows the family to move fluidly from one area and activity to another.

PREVIOUS PAGES: The home's main living level comprises two wings anchored by a double-sided, glass-walled great room, where activity and ocean views flow from the garden side to the pool and terrace side. ABOVE: An early sketch shows the concept of the home built into the hill; the diagram below envisions the corresponding layers, including the core concrete stair volume in its center. OPPOSITE: A mahogany door and protective canopy on the street level, crowned by a rooftop hedge, welcomes guests.

The street-level entry anchors the main living level above. A series of concrete, plaster, and mahogany layers and planted hedges maximize privacy.

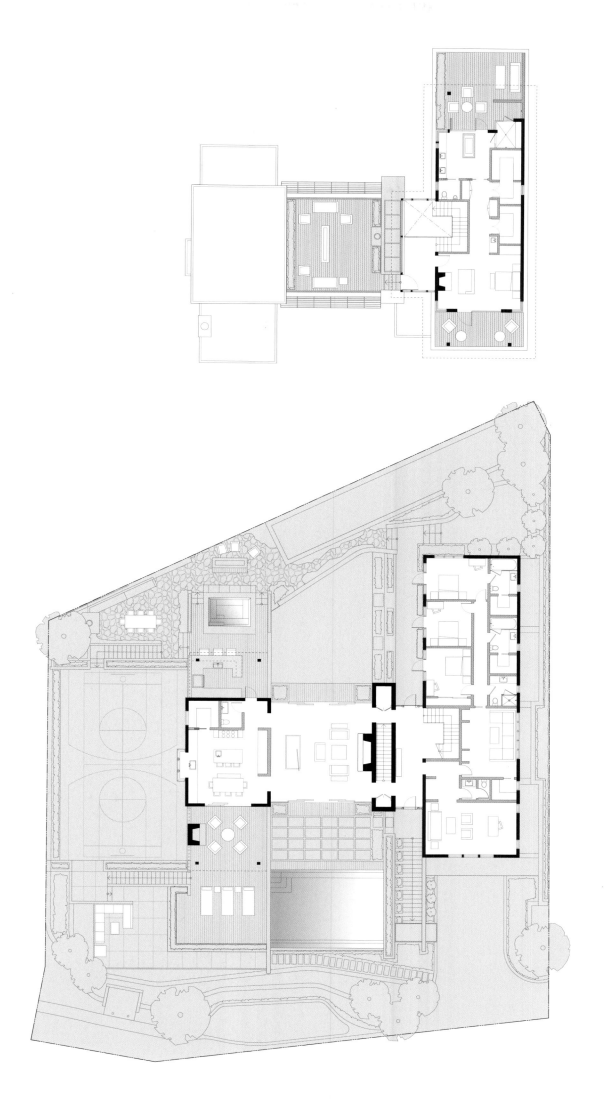

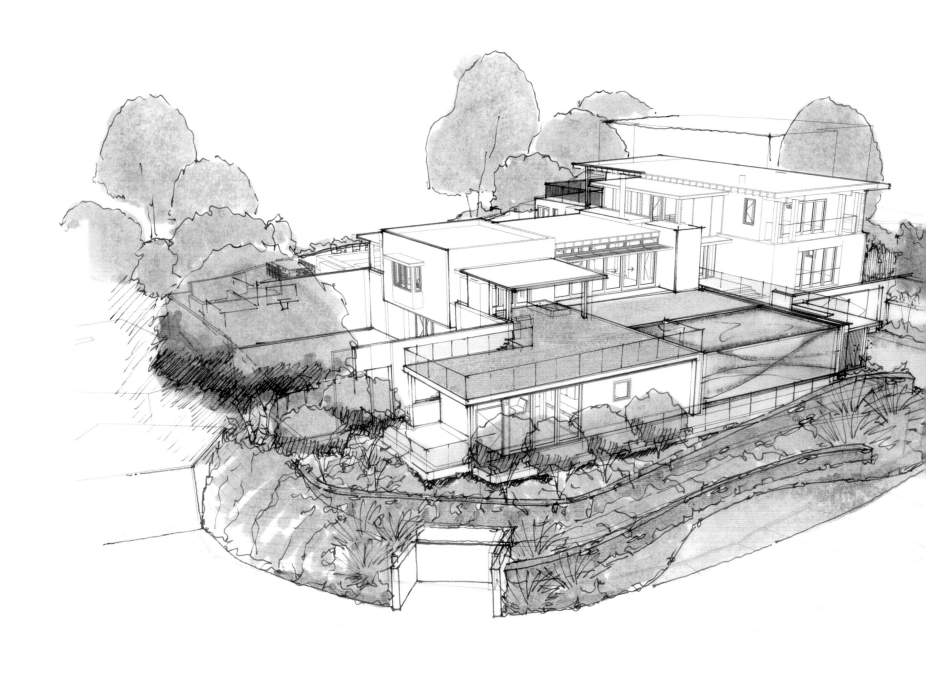

This hillside promontory was the site of the former city water tower. The three-level home is organically engaged into the sloping topography, punctuated with planted terraces and garden spaces.

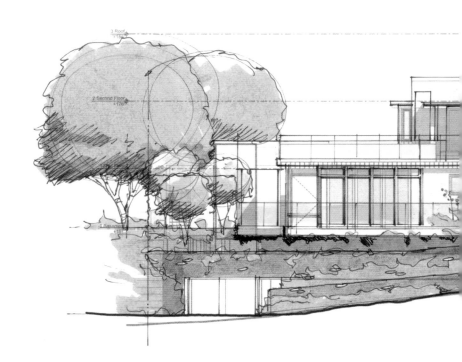

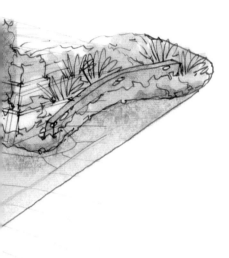

The top layer, which encompasses the private spaces, includes a master suite with its own terrace—a restful sanctuary where the couple starts the day or gathers later to enjoy the sunset. The middle layer is the living space, with a great room that anchors the family's everyday life, as well as its entertaining. Glass doors on both sides slide completely away to open the house to nature and all of the family's favorite outdoor pursuits. Right outside the great room lies the east garden, with its view over wetlands and the distant mountains. On the western side is a pool that appears to spill off into the ocean.

Having grown up in a similar hillside coastal community north of Del Mar, I felt a real kinship to this property from the start. Recalling moments from my own childhood, I was inspired to design a house that encouraged family times, friend times, fun times… while still being the compelling lookout emerging from the hill.

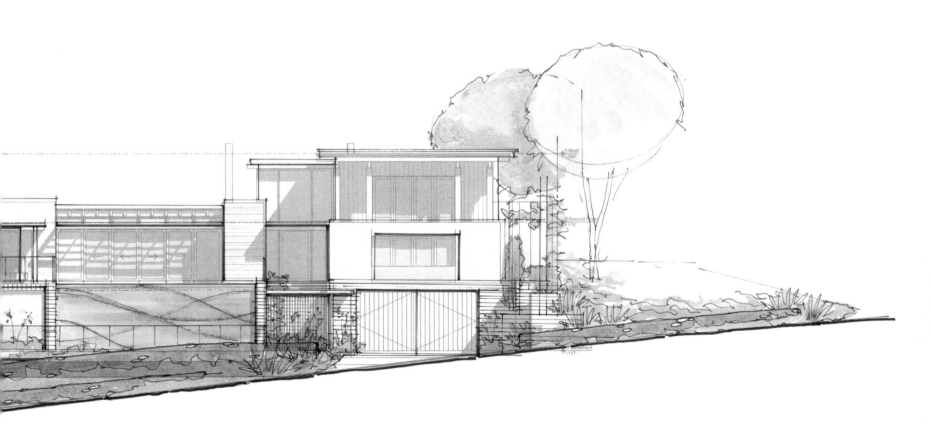

PREVIOUS PAGES: The concrete stair volume anchors the more transparent spaces, including the entry and stair foyer on the left and the great room to the right. An outdoor kitchen/bar and spa (far right) descend to a sports court beyond. OPPOSITE AND BELOW: Board-formed concrete walls and a sliding mahogany door system contribute to the indoor-outdoor flow. Crisp white plaster and teak flooring complete the warm palette of materials.

BELOW: A range of crisp, white materials complements the mahogany kitchen cabinets and teak flooring. OPPOSITE: In the three-story stair tower, sunlight filters through a skylight, accentuating the texture of the board-formed concrete walls below. FOLLOWING PAGES: The oceanside terrace offers the family multiple opportunities for entertainment. It includes a covered outdoor living room with a fireplace and television, adjacent to the kitchen; the garden and pool deck flow directly into the great room (right).

Windows abound in the top-floor master suite; paired with bifold doors, they open onto a private terrace, where the couple can survey the panorama of the town, coastline, and horizon beyond.

BELOW AND OPPOSITE: The master suite contains a spa bathroom with an indoor-outdoor shower and pocketing doors that also lead out to the private relaxation terrace. FOLLOWING PAGES: From the great room one looks across the terrace and the infinity pool, the beach town below, and the ocean beyond.

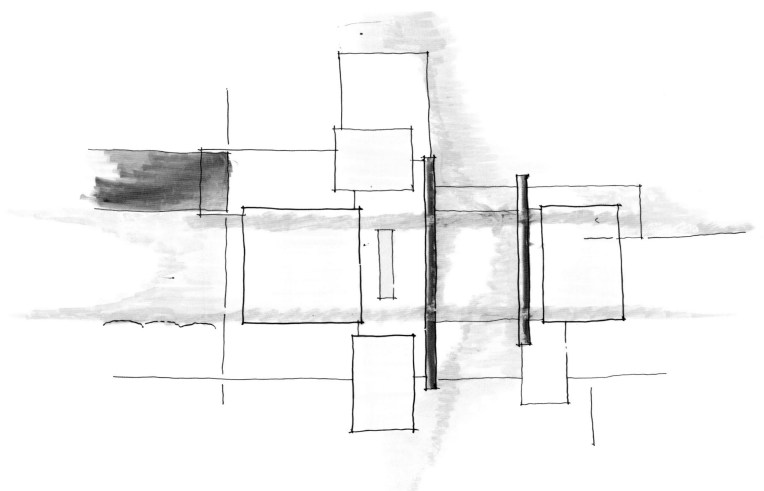

The late 1960s in Los Angeles was a prolific time for creative industries and artists, including Richard Diebenkorn, the Matisse-inspired abstract expressionist known for his *Ocean Park* series of paintings. My longtime interest in Diebenkorn's work inspired this house, which belongs to a major art collector. Diebenkorn used layers of color in an intriguing way: they seem to be adjacent, but a closer look reveals that they actually overlap. There's an emotional impact, an intimate level of connection, that emerges from those layers. Transparent turquoises dance against opaque periwinkles, and the layers switch places—approaching, then receding—under our gaze. I envisioned this home as a three-dimensional Diebenkorn painting: a house composed of vertical layers and horizontal masses, with transparent shafts of glass between them, connecting the indoors and outdoors.

At this site, two primarily flat properties were merged into one, forming a sort of bow-tie shape. The home was designed in the central knot of the bow tie, with two distinct sections opening up to the expansive grounds on either side. The site plan was

PREVIOUS PAGES: The home expands as a dance of horizontal and vertical forms separated by transparent and translucent connections. The front entry sits beneath a louvered second-floor family room and immediately connects the visitor to the expansive gardens beyond.
ABOVE: Inspired by the owner's art collection and Richard Diebenkorn's *Ocean Park* series in particular, this early concept diagram makes reference to the home as sculpture in the gardens.
OPPOSITE: In addition to framing views of the gardens, the home was designed to integrate various pieces of the owner's extensive art collection—both indoors and out. This iconic work by Anish Kapoor is a striking focal point for the living room.

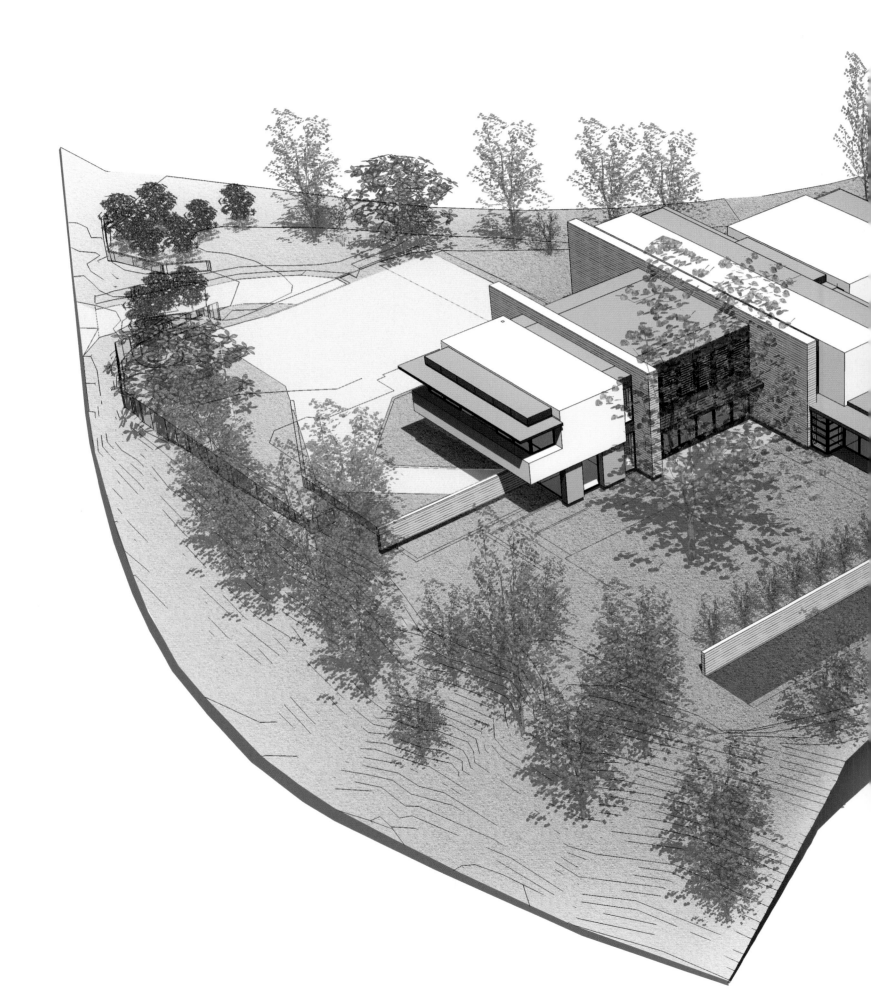

This substantial residence weaves together a varied series of gardens and outdoor entertainment and art spaces on a two-acre site. The landscaping creates a private parklike refuge in the middle of a vibrant neighborhood.

193

Large sandstone rubble walls extend from inside to outside, framing views and contrasting vertical and horizontal elements. Troweled-smooth, off-white plaster and sapele hardwood siding impart warmth and lightness.

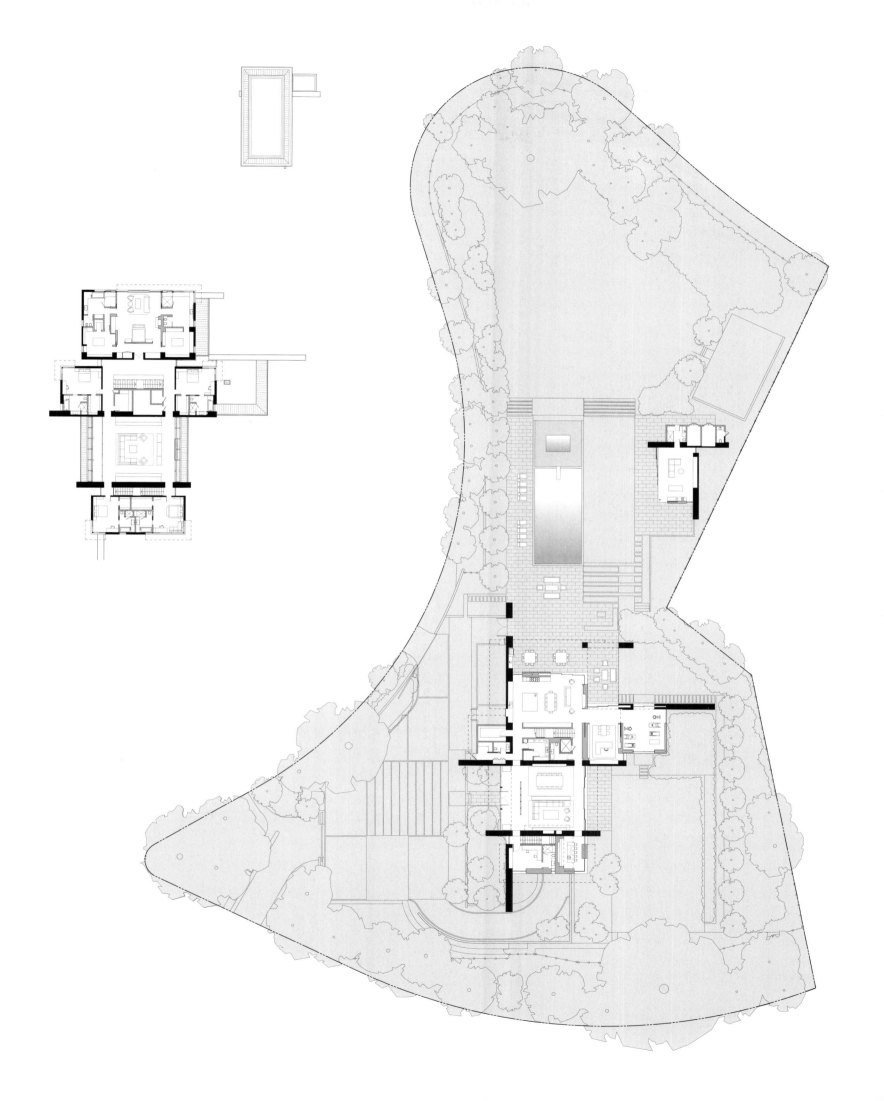

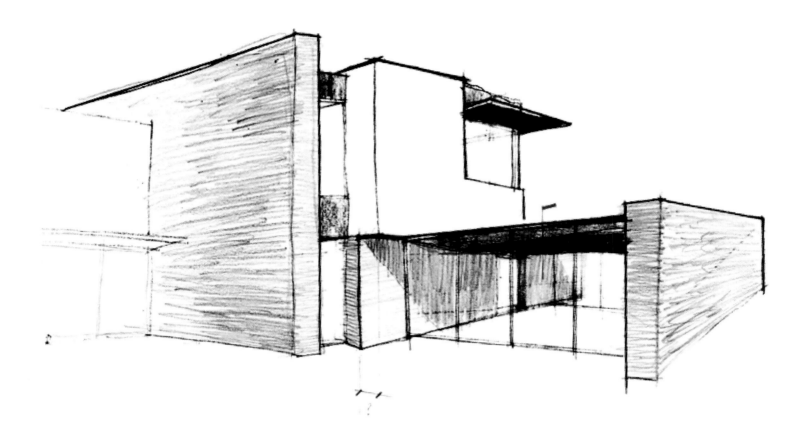

also arranged for privacy, as this house is right in the middle of Beverly Hills. Neighboring homes are not visible; instead, the house feels as though it's in the middle of a lush park, thanks to views of gardens framed through architectural portals, including the strategically placed thick walls of stone. And true to all of our work, I also created outdoor rooms where the family can appreciate the gardens and host varied events.

Inside the house, all galleries and passages offer views to the outside. Natural light abounds, and the transparent shafts between spaces infuse the interiors with the feeling of being in nature. Many of the significant walls are actually floor-to-ceiling mahogany doors that completely fold or slide away. Other walls are made of neutral plaster to highlight the art collection, featuring works from midcentury to contemporary artists.

Art and nature converse throughout the property, supporting the idea of the house as a permanent sculpture in a park. But it is the adjacencies of solid and transparent spaces and smooth and textured surfaces that create the overlap—the layers that intrigue. I like to think that Mr. Diebenkorn would have been happy here, too.

Second-story plaster volumes contain bedroom spaces with corner views to the gardens and vistas beyond. Zinc-clad window awnings shelter the large expanses of glass below.

A pool pavilion in the backyard is a beloved spot for the family and guests. A thirty-foot sliding mahogany-and-glass door system opens onto the garden and pool areas.

Central to family living is the great room, which includes kitchen, casual dining, and lounge areas that flow into generous covered outdoor entertainment areas for weekend and large-scale events.

RIGHT: The husband's master bath incorporates silver travertine floors, windows framed in mahogany, lacquered vanity cabinets, and recessed lighting in the mirrors. FOLLOWING PAGES: The master suite floats above the covered outdoor entertainment areas, which survey the pool and gardens and complete the Diebenkorn homage of home as sculpture in the garden.

BALANCE HILL

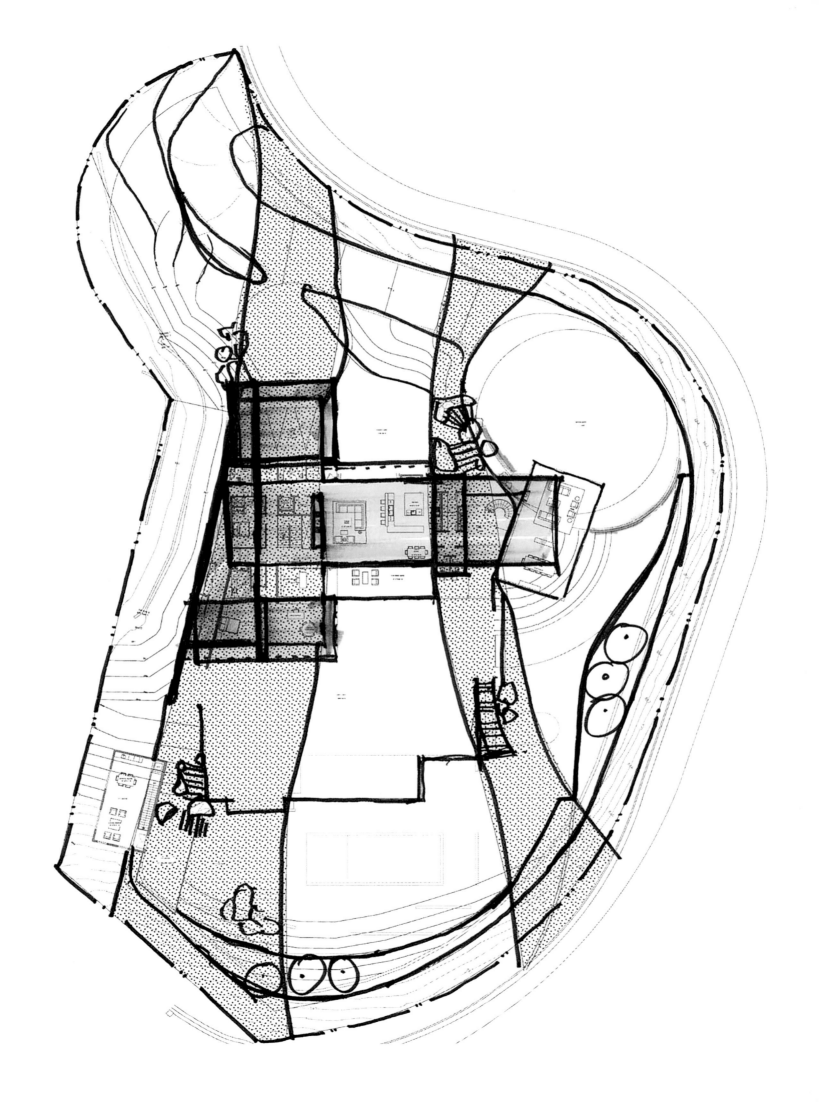

Energy. Harmony. Balance. This hillside residence was meant to make a statement by achieving a synchronicity with its location. It was inspired, in part, by the Case Study Houses (the mid-twentieth-century program sponsored by *Arts & Architecture* magazine to foster modernist home design), such as Pierre Koenig's iconic Stahl House, where views of Los Angeles shimmer through the windows of a room like a cube of ice jutting out over the hill. Here, too, I cantilevered the living room and twisted it at an angle to create an exhilarating sense of levitation for anyone inside this aerie. Throughout the residence, we incorporated opportunities for this kind of elevated experience.

While the site offered several obvious catalysts for the design—chief among them the desire to maximize the views—the clients also wanted a real family home. That meant supporting stylistic bravado with functionality and livability. We faced a challenge: when someone says "family home," I think of nice, flat grounds with sprawling lawns and gently flowing areas on hills that are not the least bit dangerous. Neither of those serene images describes the reality of the original hillside property. The solution was to build a spacious underground level with an expansive lawn on top.

Easy access to outdoor areas was important for the family, and so we designed a transparent, double-sided living space. When they're all together in the family room, large sliding glass walls allow gatherings to flow outside onto the big lawn. The other

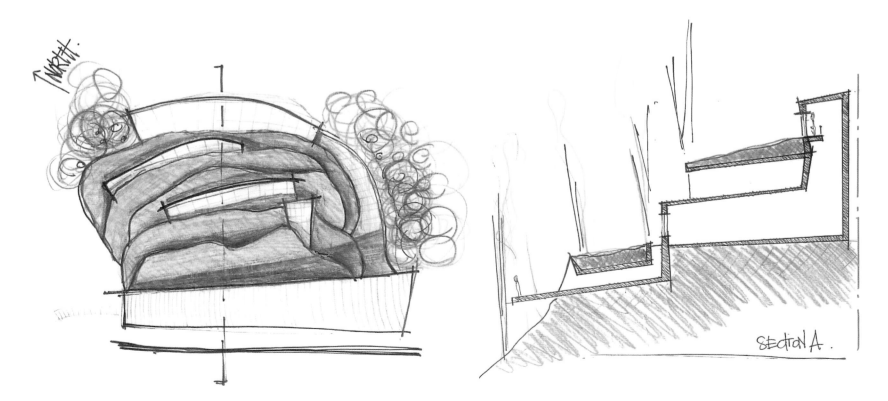

RIGHT: The first level of the home tucks into the hillside, held by curving, board-formed concrete walls. Two higher levels emerge as stacked slabs, twisted over the foundations and suspended above the property and the city beyond. FOLLOWING PAGES: Family bedrooms reside in the top level of the home, which employs a flexible system of wood, glass, and operable shutters for privacy and sun control. Glass doors and windows encase the main level, allowing vistas of sky, land, garden, and city to permeate its spaces.

view of stair from dining

side of the same room gives way to a private, protected garden. Life moves inside and out with very little effort, as do the elements.

Throughout the home, straight lines, geometric shapes, and tight corners abound. I had originally designed the site walls to fit this vernacular, as well. But something was missing. The house was predominantly orthogonal, but those walls? They needed to curve. Made of well-crafted board-formed concrete, these sinuous site walls engage the home with the hillside and help guide the eye. From the entry gate to the front door, these walls suggest motion and procession from outdoors to indoors. Suspended over the arrival court, the section of the home that contains the living area beckons as soon as visitors enter the front gate. Two curving walls then invite the visitor up to the front entry: a simple shaft between the volumes that creates the glassed-in foyer.

The idea of natural topography continues inside the house. Here, the moving line is rendered as a sinuous spiral stairway—feminine and sexy, like a stiletto or a ribbon unfurling. And the views of the city and the ocean—the undulating skyline, the water, and the hills below—extend the balance and harmony inherent in living with the world at one's feet.

A spiral stair, rendered in crisp white plaster with maple treads, makes a statement in the entry foyer. The fluid, sculptural form contrasts with the straight lines that dominate the architecture.

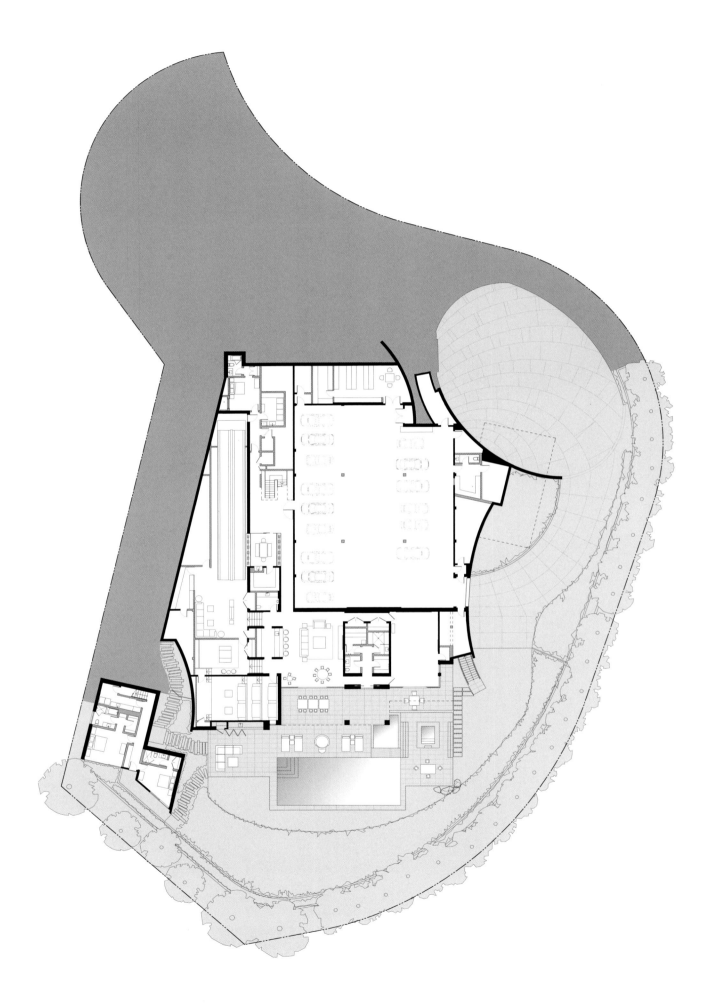

A minimal materials palette of floor-to-ceiling glass, white plaster on the ceiling, and steel columns finished in automotive paint enhances the panoramic view from the cantilevered living room.

A great room with kitchen, dining, and lounge areas centers the home. One side opens to the garden, the other to the main lawn with city views (opposite). Maple cabinetry clads the entertainment wall in the lounge under a ceiling of exterior maple siding (below).

221

Maple cabinetry set against slate stone walls gives the kitchen a serene feel. Custom designed by the interior designer, Antonia Hutt, in a burnt-orange lacquer, the breakfast table adds a vibrant note.

The main dining and adjacent living areas share the cantilevered space, maximizing the view of the cityscape below.

The lower level showcases the family's passions, pursuits, and collections,
featuring a wine room, bowling alley, home theater, and fitness rooms
and offering access to the pool, terraces, and outdoor kitchen and dining areas.

226

The main-level garden terrace floats
over the spa and fire pit areas as
it reaches for the city lights below.

TOWER GROVE

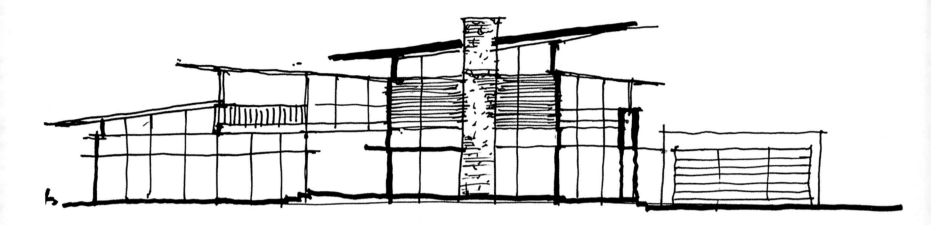

This home is an eco-village where two can live comfortably, yet it opens up grandly. Set on a plateau overlooking the sprawling city below, the residence was conceived as a series of linked pavilions interspersed with gardens and outdoor entertainment spaces. The interiors and exteriors, at a human scale to suit the couple's day-to-day lives, also accommodate their large families and the guests they frequently host for their businesses and the nonprofits they're involved in.

Both the husband and wife are in the entertainment industry, so we infused the spaces with a sense of inspiration and even playfulness. Her office is tucked back, overlooking the pool, promoting focus and contemplation, while his wood-clad office, resembling a tree house, jauntily juts out over a first-floor deck and the hillside below.

The tree house metaphor is an apt one for this couple, since they love nature and have a deep respect for the environment. We prioritized eco-conscious architecture and landscaping, from the butterfly roof that is at the ideal angle for generating solar power (and also offers a stylistic flourish of optimism and uplift) to the recirculation system that irrigates the landscape with water that would otherwise be wasted. Sustainable materials include FSC-certified wood throughout the home and even the stone for the exterior walls, which came from the property.

The husband and wife enjoy the green roofs, terrace with infinity pool, and fire pits, all of which are magnets for guests. Mahogany wall panels, floor planks, and louvered slats on windows appear throughout the house, including on those windows that look out onto a serene courtyard with the husband's beloved sculpture of three dancing pigs, a wink that expresses the humor that often fills this home. At night, these wooden slats conspire with clerestory windows and warm lighting pooling on the eaves to transform the home into a glowing lantern, extending the feeling of serenity—an invitation from a welcoming village.

PREVIOUS PAGES: The roof of the main living volume (left) and the suspended office (right) peek over the garden wall, as seen from the street below. ABOVE: An early concept sketch shows sloping roof forms that extend to capture the vistas and natural light while providing broad overhangs for shade and shelter below. OPPOSITE: A playful but important V-shaped steel structural column system supports the husband's suspended mahogany-clad office space. FOLLOWING PAGES: A modern-organic palette of materials was chosen for this eco-conscious home: stone walls, mahogany siding and details, and board-formed concrete walls. A majestic California oak tree is the centerpiece of the motor court.

ABOVE: A modern take on the post-and-beam architecture prevalent in the early twentieth century is envisioned in this early concept sketch. The village-like assemblage, including the wife's office wing on the far left and the husband's cantilevered office wing on the far right, emerged at the very beginning of the process and remained fundamental to the design. FOLLOWING PAGES, LEFT: Expert craftsmanship included an intricate level of refinement in the exterior of the house. Ease of maintenance lends itself to more enjoyment by the residents: the louvered shutter system is removable for easy window cleaning and occasional wood care. FOLLOWING PAGES, RIGHT: A two-story mahogany column supports the butterfly-shape roof, which extends toward the panorama of the city below.

The abundant colors of sky
and foliage inspired the
architecture and landscape
design. A rooftop garden of
native grasses above the
wife's office wing reinforces
this connection.

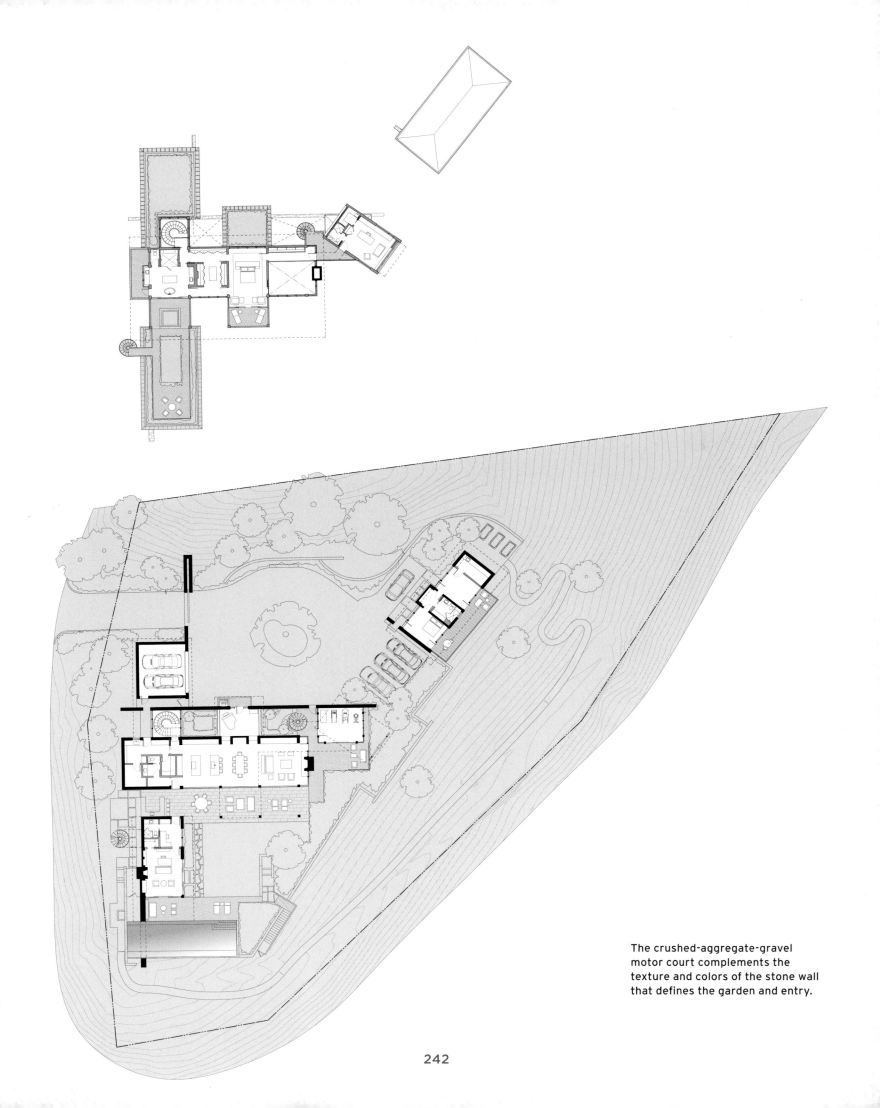

The crushed-aggregate-gravel
motor court complements the
texture and colors of the stone wall
that defines the garden and entry.

BELOW, LEFT: Tucked between garden spaces, a curved mahogany and steel stair ascends to the master suite above. BELOW, RIGHT, AND OPPOSITE: An interior bridge connects the master suite to the husband's office, across the double-height living room. Expertly crafted wood and stonework marry rusticity and refinement.

Kitchen, dining, and living spaces join as one and unfold onto the adjacent covered outdoor terrace. The two-story living room stone fireplace anchors the interior.

The open kitchen features teak wood cabinetry and floors, stone countertops, and a custom stainless-steel rack above.

BELOW: The wife's office incorporates board-formed concrete and mahogany cabinets. Clerestory windows surround the room, grazing the ceiling with light during the day and setting the eaves aglow outside at night. OPPOSITE: The pool slips through a portal in the concrete wall, emphasizing the indoor-outdoor layers that epitomize this home. FOLLOWING PAGES: The residents' love of nature is expressed in the symbiotic design of their residence.

ACKNOWLEDGMENTS

This book—everything about this book—comes from the vibrant organism called the KAA Design Group. I am most proud of the word *Group*, for without this talented team of the last thirty years, there is no book, and no KAA. In 1988 I rather foolishly left a good job and started Kirkpatrick Associates Architects. A few years later, when it was apparent I wouldn't be doing this on my own, I took the name off the door and the firm became known as KAA. It's the greatest team I have ever been on; when I think of those three letters, I think of talent first—crazy talent. And then hard work, dedication, and pride. I love all you KAAers: this book is testament to your collective spirit and endless creativity, and I am honored to be on your team.

To my partners, Erik Evens and Duan Tran, you inspire me daily to keep the pedal down and focus on beauty. To Patti Baker, Steve Straughan, Lisa Copeland, Michael McGowan, and Megan Beckmann, with your collective *one hundred-plus* years of KAA torchbearing, your leadership and challenge drive us to do incredible things.

I come from a family who appreciates beauty as an essential human trait. To my father, Robert, Mr. Green Thumb, whom my brothers and I spent hours in the gardens with: I didn't know it at the time, but you passed along the gift of seeing nature as beauty—and there is no greater gift. To my mother, Nadine, whose strong but angelic voice reverberated beauty throughout our home: I thank you for my creative DNA and chutzpah. To my brothers, Gregg and Kent, I am grateful for our comradery and competitive spirit and for you forcing your architect brother to take business classes. To my kids, Jack, Ryan, and Allie: I thank you for rolling around in the dirt with me and making life worthwhile. And to my wife, Shaya: our love is what makes it all work. I told you years ago that I have two loves; you said you would be OK with that. You have supported and nurtured my love for this crazy profession from the beginning, and you have never stopped. I remain forever grateful for the day I met you.

The making of this book has been a challenging but exciting adventure. I am grateful to Jill Cohen for helping to craft this unusual book and for connecting me to Kevin Lippert, Jennifer Lippert, Sara Stemen, and the rest of the team at Princeton Architectural Press, who saw the value of such an idea early on and helped to execute its countless incarnations. Crucial to that process have been our book designers, Doug Turshen and David Huang, and writers, Nancy Greystone in Los Angeles and Aliza Fogelson in New

York. I am very thankful for the positive energy and countless hours of my own KAA book team, especially John Margolis, our amazing Joyce Lopez, and my thirty-year colleague at KAA, Steve Straughan.

Key to these projects and KAA's success is our close network of design and construction collaborators. All of these important team members have joined us on multiple endeavors herein, and we trust and value their contributions to these and our forthcoming sanctuaries. For interior design, they include Terry Hunziker, Victoria Hagan, Tim Clarke, Alana Homesley, Mark Williams, Antonia Hutt, Chris Barrett, Deborah Rumens and Mike Lee, Taylor Borsari, Joan Behnke, Doug Durkin, and Suzanne Ascher. For landscape architecture, they include Bob Truskowski, Jerry Williams, John Feldman, Nancy Power, Pamela Burton, and my talented and dear friend Damon Hein. For construction, they include Shawn Nelson, Dave Baldwin, David Garinger, Peter McCoy, Rick Holz, Dan McGee, Jeff Wilson, George Minardos, Matt Morris, Chris Lombardi, David Cohen, Ron Johns, Matt Wachtfogel, and Terry Wardell. And we are deeply indebted to Dave McCarroll and his team at KGM Architectural Lighting for twenty-five years of gracefully bringing forth the light, in and out of our homes.

This book celebrates thirty years of design by KAA, but key people have played a major role in helping to define the company in critical capacities beyond the design of our projects. They include Craig Yabuki, Bryn Stroyke, Joyce Rey, Susân Perryman, Meg Touborg, Erik Perez, Elizabeth Fortune, and, of course, Keith Granet, who has been an essential contributor to all things KAA and a dear friend.

I have learned that 99 percent of people who see our work do so only through the lens of the photographer. I am deeply grateful to have worked and continue to work so closely with the best of the best: Roger Davies, Sharon Risedorph, Tim Street-Porter, Erhard Pfeiffer, Farshid Assassi, Joe Fletcher, Karyn Millet, Lisa Romerein, Manolo Langis, Weldon Brewster, and Richard Powers.

And to my mentors, Bruce Meyer and Steven Spierer: I give you hugs and thanks for the bread crumbs and for being in my life.

And to each of our passionate clients who have entrusted us with the task of helping them pursue dreams: I feel fortunate to have earned your trust and to call you visionaries and true friends.

Grant Camden Kirkpatrick

PROJECT CREDITS

SHIPSHAPE (PAGES 126-45)
INTERIOR DESIGNER: Douglas Durkin Design
CONTRACTOR: Matt Morris Development / I-Grace
LIGHTING DESIGNER: KGM Architectural Lighting
LANDSCAPE ARCHITECT: KAA Design Group

SAND STREETS (PAGES 146-65)
INTERIOR DESIGNER: Owner
CONTRACTOR: Lombardi Construction
LIGHTING DESIGNER: KGM Architectural Lighting
LANDSCAPE ARCHITECT: KAA Design Group

PACIFIC BELVEDERE (PAGES 166-87)
INTERIOR DESIGNER: Mark J. Williams Design
CONTRACTOR: Wardell Builders
LIGHTING DESIGNER: KGM Architectural Lighting
LANDSCAPE ARCHITECT: KAA Design Group

EN PLEIN AIR (PAGES 188-205)
INTERIOR DESIGNER: Chinese Jesus
CONTRACTOR: Finton Construction
LIGHTING DESIGNER: KGM Architectural Lighting
LANDSCAPE ARCHITECT: KAA Design Group

BALANCE HILL (PAGES 206-29)
INTERIOR DESIGNER: Antonia Hutt & Associates
CONTRACTOR: Richard Holz Inc.
LIGHTING DESIGNER: KGM Architectural Lighting
LANDSCAPE ARCHITECT: KAA Design Group /
Robert E. Truskowski Landscape Architects

TOWER GROVE (PAGES 230-59)
INTERIOR DESIGNER: Tim Clarke Design
CONTRACTOR: Davis Development Group
LIGHTING DESIGNER: The Ruzika Company
LANDSCAPE ARCHITECT: KAA Design Group

PHOTOGRAPHY CREDITS

Farshid Assassi: 34-37, 47, 63 top left, 71, 93, 101

Roger Davies: front cover, 6, 33, 38, 42, 43 top left, 54-55, 60-62, 63 top right, 74-75, 86, 88, 96-97, 102-3, 104 top right, 106, 110-13, 121, 146-47, 149-51, 153-55, 158-65, 166-67, 169-70, 174-87

Joe Fletcher: 234-35, 238, back endpaper

Manolo Langis: back cover, 2-3, 6, 43 top right and bottom left, 46, 48 all, 50-53, 63 bottom right, 64-69, 72-73, 76-79, 85, 87 all, 90-91, 94-95, 99, 104 top left and bottom left, 105, 114-17, 120 bottom left and bottom right, 125-28, 130-32, 134-37, 139-45, 206-7, 210-13, 215, 218-19, 222-23, 227, 230-31, 233, 239-41, 243-53

Karyn Millet: 17, 56-57, 104 bottom right, 118-19

Michael Misczynski: 49 right

Erhard Pfeiffer: 43 bottom right, 107, 120 top right

Richard Powers: 220, 224-26, 228-29

Sharon Risedorph: 39, 40-41, 44-45, 58-59, 63 bottom left, 80-81, 89, 92, 100, 108-9, 120 top left, 122-23

Lisa Romerein: front endpaper, 8-9, 11-14, 19-31

Tim Street-Porter: 188-89, 191, 194, 197-205

Noah Webb: 49 left, 82-83

Published by
Princeton Architectural Press
A McEvoy Group company
202 Warren Street
Hudson, New York 12534
Visit our website at www.papress.com.

Princeton Architectural Press is a leading publisher in architecture, design, photography, landscape, and visual culture. We create fine books and stationery of unsurpassed quality and production values. With more than one thousand titles published, we find design everywhere and in the most unlikely places.

Editor: Sara Stemen
Designer: Doug Turshen with David Huang

Special thanks to: Ryan Alcazar, Janet Behning, Nolan Boomer, Abby Bussel, Benjamin English, Jan Cigliano Hartman, Susan Hershberg, Kristen Hewitt, Lia Hunt, Valerie Kamen, Jennifer Lippert, Sara McKay, Eliana Miller, Nina Pick, Wes Seeley, Rob Shaeffer, Marisa Tesoro, Paul Wagner, and Joseph Weston of Princeton Architectural Press
—Kevin C. Lippert, publisher

Library of Congress Cataloging-in-Publication Data
Names: Kirkpatrick, Grant Camden, author.
Title: California contemporary : the Houses of Grant C. Kirkpatrick and KAA Design / Grant C. Kirkpatrick.
Description: First edition. | Hudson, New York : Princeton Architectural Press, 2018.
Identifiers: LCCN 2017035832 | ISBN 9781616896584 (hardback)
Subjects: LCSH: Kirkpatrick, Grant Camden—Themes, motives. | KAA Design Group. | Architect-designed houses—California. | BISAC: ARCHITECTURE / Individual Architects & Firms / Monographs.
Classification: LCC NA737.K56 A4 2018 | DDC 728/.3709794—dc23
LC record available at https://lccn.loc.gov/2017035832